All About Faith

Book Two
Foundations of Religion

Anne Boyle and Niall Boyle

Gill & Macmillan

Gill & Macmillan Ltd
Hume Avenue
Park West
Dublin 12
with associated companies throughout the world
www.gillmacmillan.ie

© Anne and Niall Boyle 2001

0 7171 2973 X
Print origination in Ireland by Carole Lynch
Imprimatur: Most Rev. Michael Smith DCL, Bishop of Meath

The paper used in this book is made from the wood pulp of managed forests. For every tree felled, at least one tree is planted, thereby renewing natural resources.

Photo Acknowledgments
Many thanks to the following for allowing us to reproduce images in this book: The Art Archive; Circa Photo Library; Anne & Bury Peerless; the Science Photo Library; Robert Harding Pictures; Slide File; the Bridgeman Photo Library; Frank Spooner Pictures; Mary Evans Picture Library; AKG; Corbis; PA Photos; Robin Bryant; Scala; Lisa Taylor; MSM; and the Natural History Museum Photo Library.

Contents

Part One

Exploring Religion

CHAPTER ONE

RELIGION IN TODAY'S WORLD

Introduction

Just consider:

■ Religion has been one of the most powerful forces in human history. Its origins have been traced as far back as 60,000 years ago. Its teachings have shaped the lives of countless people ever since.

■ Many people live by religion and some are even prepared to die for it.

■ Some men and women are so inspired by religion that they will travel to the most inhospitable places on earth, to help ease the sufferings of their fellow human beings, because of it.

■ Over the centuries religion has divided many people, but it has brought even more people closer together, by making them aware of how much they share in common with each other.

■ Religion has been abused by some to do harm to others and to excuse violence. It has also, however, been a great force for good, by providing hope and encouragement for all those who want to make the world a better place.

■ When people are faced with situations where they think that they have reached the limits of their endurance, they can draw strength from religion to go on.

■ Religion has been the inspiration for many magnificent buildings and beautiful works of art.

■ Religion can be found, in one form or other, in every part of the globe. It is central to the way in which most human beings live their lives.

Interior of the Sistine Chapel, Rome.
▼

The Presence of Religion

Hindus

▲
Hindus washing themselves in the river Ganges.

It is midday on Friday. High in the icy mountains of the Himalayas in northern India, a group of weary travellers have finally reached their destination. They have stopped just above the snowline. They have made the long and difficult journey from the hot and dusty plains below for a reason. They have come here to find the birthplace of the mighty river Ganges. They believe that this is the holiest place on earth. They consider the river Ganges to be the source of life and energy in this land of heat and dust. In this beautiful but freezing landscape, these people will wash themselves in its icy waters as a sign that they want the goddess Ganga to wash away all the wrong things they have done in the past. They are *Hindus*. They belong to the oldest of the world's great religions and share their beliefs with seven hundred and fifty million others.

Christians

It is midday on Friday. A cool breeze flows along Fifth Avenue, New York City, offering some welcome relief from the scorching summer sun. As usual, this broad, skyscraper-lined street is packed with shoppers and sightseers. However, not everyone is intent on queuing to see the view from the top of the Empire State building, or on buying an expensive jacket in a big department store. Some people have a different destination in mind. They are on their way to St Patrick's Cathedral, a massive, gothic-style church. They enter through its huge bronze doors. They are just in time. Mass is about to begin. These people are *Catholics*. They have chosen to give up their lunch hour to meet with one another, to pray together and to give thanks as a community to God. They are only the tiniest part of Christianity, the world's most widespread and, with two billion members, largest religion.

Muslims

It is midday on Friday. The normally bustling market-place of the old city of Kairouan in Tunisia has fallen silent. A group of Western holiday-makers, their shopping and sightseeing over, board their coach to continue their tour. These tourists are so busy chatting amongst themselves and enjoying the coach's air-conditioning after the intense heat of the city's streets, that they fail to hear the call which echoes from the square tower of a fortress-like building across from them.

This building is a *mosque* (i.e. house of prayer) for *Muslims*, i.e. the followers of *Islam*. The call is given by the *muezzin*. He announces that it is now time for Muslims to pray. Friday is the Muslim holy day.

At midday every Friday, over one-and-a-quarter billion Muslims across the globe unfold their prayer rugs, face the holy city of Mecca in Saudi Arabia and repeat the words:

Allahu Akbar. Allahu Akbar. Meaning: God is greatest. God is greatest.

Jews

It is midday on Friday. The city of Jerusalem in Israel is thronged with people going about their daily business. A young boy accompanies his father through the narrow streets. They leave the hustle and bustle of the crowded shopping districts behind and join a group of people gathered in the large, open forecourt of one of the city's most famous sites. But they are not here to admire an ancient monument. They are *Jews*. They have come here to pray. This is the place where the great Temple once stood.

Only one part of the Temple complex now remains. This is known as the Western or 'Wailing' Wall, so-called because for centuries Jews have come to this place to pray and to mourn the Temple's destruction by the Roman army in A.D. 70. For eighteen million Jews, this is a holy place.

Jew praying at the Western Wall, Jerusalem. ➡

Buddhists

It is midday on Friday. The city of Bangkok in Thailand, one of South-East Asia's most-popular tourist destinations, is sweltering in the summer sun. The city centre is clogged with slow-moving traffic.

Buddhist monks.

Frustrated motorists blare their car horns in the vain hope that this will somehow encourage those in front of them to move more quickly. Adding to the noisy hum of the city is the excited bargaining between shoppers and the stall-holders who line the sidewalks. Through all this noise and confusion, a small group of young men, dressed in yellow robes, quietly makes its way, walking in single file. As a sign that they attach no importance to worldly goods, the men walk barefoot along the hot stone pavements. They humbly hold out begging bowls hoping that they will be given a few handfuls of rice with which to feed themselves. They are rarely disappointed. They are usually treated generously. They are *Buddhist* monks. They share their beliefs with three hundred and fifty million others. Though mostly to be found in South-East Asia, there are also Buddhist communities in Western Europe and North America.

Reflection – Religious Creatures?

As we can see, most people in today's world believe in a God or gods of some kind. What they believe about God is called their *religion* or *faith*.

There are many different religions. They all started in different places, at different times and in different ways. However, all of these religions exert a powerful influence over the lives of billions of people across the globe.

It seems that, wherever there are people, so too you will find *some* sort of religion.

It has been said that human beings are by nature *religious creatures*. Like art and technology, religion is one of the things that makes human beings different from other creatures on our planet. Why this is so and what difference it makes are questions we shall explore in this book.

QUESTIONS

1. Name each of the five religions mentioned in this section.
2. Which is the *largest* of the world's great religions?
3. Which is the *oldest* of the world's great religions?
4. What is a mosque?
5. What does the Muslim prayer *'Allahu Akbar'* mean?
6. What day of the week is the Muslim holy day?
7. What day of the week is the Christian holy day?
8. What major event in Jewish history occurred in A.D. 70?
9. What is the name given to the remaining section of the Temple complex in Jerusalem?
10. Why do Buddhist monks dress simply, beg for food and walk barefoot?
11. What does it mean to say that human beings are by nature *religious creatures*?

JOURNAL WORK

What aspects of your religion strike you as being
(a) the same as other religions and
(b) different from other religions?

CHAPTER TWO

THE MEANING OF MYSTERY

Introduction

In order to have a clear understanding of the role religion plays in people's lives, we need to understand the difference between the words *problem* and *mystery*.

In everyday conversation, the word *mystery* is often confused with the word *problem*. There are, however, important differences between the two.

What is a problem?

■ It is a question that has an *answer*, even if no one knows what it is yet.

■ It is a puzzle which can be completely *solved*, though it may take much time and effort to do so.

What is a mystery?

■ It is a question that *cannot* be answered for once and for all, because the matter it explores is so vast and deep in meaning that it can never be fully explained.

■ It is a puzzle which *cannot* be completely solved though a person may gain insights and grow in understanding of it.

How can we tell a problem from a mystery? Something may appear to be a problem but really be a mystery or vice versa.

Let us now turn to consider a well-known historical incident that is frequently referred to as a *mystery of the high seas*, and see how this can help us to distinguish *problem* from *mystery*.

The Strange Case of the Mary Celeste

At 1pm on 5 December 1872, a crewman on watch aboard the British merchant sailing ship *Dei Gratia* caught sight of another vessel that seemed to be in distress. Their position was half way between the Portuguese coast and the Azores in the eastern Atlantic.

Captain David Morehouse of the *Dei Gratia* became convinced that something was very wrong. The unidentified sailing ship in the distance seemed to alter its course every time the wind changed direction. Suspecting its steering system might be damaged, Morehouse ordered his own vessel to alter course to offer help.

As the *Dei Gratia* came alongside the unidentified ship, Captain Morehouse could not see anyone on its deck. He called out on the loud hailer. No one responded. He ordered a lifeboat to be lowered and he took a small, three-man search party to investigate.

As the lifeboat drew alongside, Morehouse could read the name on the ship's bows – *Mary Celeste.* Looking upwards as they climbed aboard, each man wondered what horrors would greet them. Had the crew of the ship been struck down by disease? Had there been a mutiny?

Morehouse and his men hauled themselves over the ship's rails and dropped onto the deck. They were quite unprepared for what they found. The deck was completely deserted. Save for the noise of the wind in the sails and the eerie creaking of the ship's timbers, there was not a sound. There was no sign of any fighting, no traces of blood. The ship's wheel was spinning freely.

The search party went through the *Mary Celeste* from stem to stern. The ship's lifeboat and navigational instruments were missing, but its cargo of industrial alcohol was intact. Of Captain Benjamen Briggs, his wife, their daughter, and the seven other crew members, there was no trace.

The search party was puzzled by *one curious fact*. All the hatches, which should have covered the access points from the ship's deck to the compartments below, were scattered about the deck, almost as if they had been *blown off*.

Captain Briggs' last log entry was dated 24 November 1872. He recorded the *Mary Celeste's* position as six hundred and fifty km west of where the *Dei Gratia's* crew had found her. What possible reason could an experienced ship's captain like Briggs have had for abandoning his ship and loading his family and crew into a small and comparatively unstable lifeboat? Although there was evidence that the *Mary Celeste* had recently weathered a storm, the ship was seaworthy. In fact, it was in better condition than most of the vessels then regularly plying the Atlantic routes.

Captain Morehouse left his first mate Oliver Deveau and two sailors on board and both ships sailed on to Gibraltar, where a naval court could not reach a satisfactory conclusion about the fate of the crew of the *Mary Celeste*... .

QUESTIONS

1. Imagine that you are a member of the *Dei Gratia's* search party. Describe what you found when you went aboard the *Mary Celeste*.

2. What was the *one curious fact* that puzzled the search party?

▼ Map of *Mary Celeste's* route.

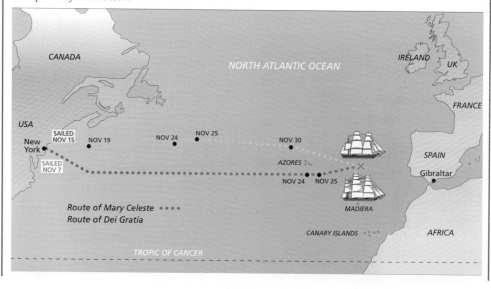

Theories

Over the years since the discovery of the *Mary Celeste* adrift in the eastern Atlantic, different solutions have been offered to explain the disappearance of its crew:

1. Murder?

Did the *Mary Celeste's* crew gain access to its cargo of alcohol, murder Captain Briggs, and then abandon ship?

No. The cargo was *denatured* alcohol. Anyone who drank it would have suffered from severe pains long before he could have become drunk.

2. Piracy?

Did Captain Morehouse and the crew of the *Dei Gratia* board the *Mary Celeste* and then murder its crew?

There is no evidence whatsoever to support this. A court in London shortly afterwards cleared Morehouse and his crew of any suspicion.

3. Attack by a sea monster?

The early twentieth century favoured stories in which the *Mary Celeste* was attacked by a giant squid that plucked the entire crew off its deck.

Even though such creatures do exist, it is highly unlikely that everyone aboard the *Mary Celeste* would have obligingly stayed on deck and allowed the monster to pluck them off one by one.

4. Abduction?

Were the *Mary Celeste's* crew abducted by a UFO?

There is no evidence currently available to support the idea that alien beings have ever visited our world.

5. Insanity?

Was the food or drinking water aboard the *Mary Celeste* contaminated? Did it cause the crew to go beserk?

No. The *Dei Gratia's* first mate, Oliver Deveau and the other crewmen used the food and water they found aboard the *Mary Celeste*. They suffered no ill effects.

6. Threat of explosion?

The cargo of denatured alcohol in the *Mary Celeste's* hold was an explosive mixture. Did this cargo give off fumes which were mistaken for smoke and lead the crew to think that the *Mary Celeste* was about to be blown out of the water?

No. This cargo would not have given off any visible vapour. There would have been no warning if it was about to explode. The cargo was intact when Captain Morehouse of the *Dei Gratia* later checked it.

COMMENT

Having examined the six theories outlined above it is not surprising that so many people considered the disappearance of the *Mary Celeste's* crew to be a *mystery* rather than a *problem*.

No solution offered so far seems to account for *all* the circumstances, but it is possible to list some facts that might provide a few clues:

■ The *Mary Celeste* was abandoned by her captain and crew; those who abandoned ship did so in its lifeboat. This small vessel would have been overloaded and easily capsized.

■ The ship was abandoned in a hurry: extra clothing was not taken nor – as far as is known – any food or water. However, the crew did not abandon ship in complete panic, since they took time to collect navigational books and instruments.

■ Since there is no evidence that the *Mary Celeste* had suffered any damage, whatever made the crew abandon her was either something they feared *had happened* or *was about to happen*, but clearly *never did*.

Case Solved?

Theory

Dr James H Kimble, former head of the US Weather Bureau in New York, has suggested that the *Mary Celeste* was struck by a *waterspout*, i.e. a tornado-like column of whirling wind and water that can appear without warning, last for up to an hour, and then break up as quickly as it has appeared.

Against

Waterspouts are not common outside the Tropics, nor is it common for ships to be struck by them.

For

■ Waterspouts have been seen outside the Tropics. For example, in December 1920 about 20 waterspouts were sighted in the English Channel.

■ A small and harmless waterspout, narrow and travelling at an angle, could have struck the *Mary Celeste* without doing a great deal of damage; indeed it would have left the vessel no worse than had she encountered a storm. This is consistent with the description of the *Mary Celeste* when first sighted by the *Dei Gratia* and would explain why all the *Mary Celeste's* hatch covers were strewn around the deck.

■ Within a waterspout the air pressure is extremely low and, as the spout passed over the ship, the marked difference in air pressure between the inside and the outside of the ship could have caused its hatch covers to blow off, in the same way that a building's walls explode *outward* when they are struck by a tornado.

■ Given this background, the method by which the *Mary Celeste* was *sounded* (i.e. checked to make sure it was not leaking) is important. This was done by dropping a rod down its pump well to measure the amount of water in the ship's hold, in much the same way as a modern motorist checks the amount of oil in his car's engine with a dipstick.

■ The drop in air pressure could have driven water from the bottom of the ship's hold up the pump well, where a valve would have prevented it from returning immediately down to the hold. Although this malfunction would have only lasted a few minutes, the crew would probably not have realised this.

■ Suppose then, that after the waterspout had passed on, the crew were left shaken and confused. Someone went to sound the ship to see if she had suffered any underwater damage. To his horror he found that the *Mary Celeste* had leaked between six and eight feet of water in less than a minute – or so he would have thought when he removed the sounding rod. Believing the *Mary Celeste* to be sinking fast, Captain Briggs may have given the order to abandon ship. This proved to be a terrible mistake.

Conclusion

The *waterspout* theory seems to fit all of the reported circumstances.

The tragic disappearance of the *Mary Celeste's* crew only appeared to be a *mystery*, while all the time it was really a *problem*. All it needed was for someone, like Dr Kimble, who had the necessary knowledge, skills and insight, to carefully examine this *case* and finally *solve it*.

QUESTIONS

1. Why was the crew's disappearance considered to be a mystery rather than a problem for many years?
2. What have you learned about the difference between a problem and a mystery? Explain your answer.

The Meaning of Mystery

Over the centuries, brilliant and gifted people have shown that many of the things which were once considered mysteries were really *problems* that could be *solved*. For example:

■ Once it was thought impossible for human beings to fly. Now we can cross oceans in a few hours by airliner, because we have discovered *how* to fly. People have even journeyed to the Moon and back.

- Once people were mystified by the strange shapes that they found in rocks. Many believed that they were the remains of dragons. Now we know they are the fossilised remains of dinosaurs that lived on Earth more than sixty-five million years ago.

- Once people were frightened by lightning flashes. Now we understand electricity and have used this knowledge to provide light, heat and power to homes and workplaces.

- Once people died from the simplest illnesses. Now doctors have discovered ways to cure an amazing number of diseases and there will be more medical breakthroughs announced in the years ahead.

Despite all this wonderful progress, however, human beings are still confronted by many important questions:

- What does it mean to be a human being?
- What is the point of our lives?
- How can a person find true happiness?
- Why do some people have to endure much harder and more tragic lives than others?
- What happens when we die?

These questions point to some of the greatest and most challenging of life's *mysteries*. Although such questions cannot be completely answered, human

God is the source of all love and wisdom.

beings can grow in their understanding of them, and gain *partial* answers.

Three religions – Judaism, Christianity and Islam – teach that human beings do *not* have to struggle on their own as they try to understand life's mysteries. They believe that beyond the world of the senses (i.e. what can be heard, seen or touched) there is *Someone* who offers human beings guidance as they struggle to find answers to life's greatest questions. This source of all wisdom is called *God*. Indeed, God is the greatest mystery of all, because though we can learn much about God we can *never* reach a point where we know everything about God.

How human beings should relate to God and deal with the mysteries of life are the central concerns of *religion*.

QUESTIONS

1. What are the great questions or mysteries of life that human beings must face?
2. What is meant by *the world of the senses?*
3. What do Jews, Christians, and Muslims believe God offers human beings?
4. Why is God referred to as *the greatest mystery of all?*
5. What are *the central concerns of religion?*

JOURNAL WORK

Select three of what you consider to be life's mysteries and explore how you might respond to them.

CHAPTER THREE

THE NATURE OF RELIGION

The Meaning of Religion

Most religions are either *monotheistic* (i.e. teach that there is only one God) or *polytheistic* (i.e. teach that there are many gods).

The precise origin of the word *religion* is uncertain, but it is thought to have come from two Latin words – *religio* meaning *reverence* and *religare* meaning *to tie* or *to link*.

At the very heart of religion is the belief that all human beings should show genuine *reverence* (i.e. loving respect) for God by leading good lives.

When people choose themselves, to think and live this way, *then* religion can act as a *link:*

- A link between God and human beings by encouraging people to grow closer to God.

- A link between people who share the same set of *beliefs* (i.e. things they accept as being true) about God.

- A link between the past and the present – by passing on these important beliefs from one generation to the next.

For genuinely religious people, their beliefs are *not* merely some added extra to their everyday life. Rather, their religion is *central* to their whole way of living and they try to put its teachings into practice in their everyday lives.

QUESTIONS

1. Explain the meaning of the following kinds of religion:
   a. *monotheistic*
   b. *polytheistic*.
2. What is the origin of the word *religion*?
3. Explain the meaning of the word *reverence*.
4. How do people show their reverence for God?
5. State the three ways in which religion can act as a *link*.

When did it begin?

▲ Early human burial.

The precise time when people began to practise religion is not known. However, archaeologists have shown that it started very early in human history.

- Excavations in the Shanidar caves of Iraq have revealed that, over sixty thousand years ago, our early human ancestors held funeral ceremonies. They buried their dead with a few possessions and left offerings of food which they thought the deceased person would need in the afterlife. These people seem to have believed in some form of life after death, which is an important part of all religions.

- Later, when humans like ourselves appeared, they too left traces of their religious beliefs. Small statues carved from either stone or mammoth ivory have been found at sites dotted across Europe. The most famous is the so-called *Venus of Willendorf* which was made about twenty five thousand years ago. This little carved statue suggests that many early humans may have worshipped a mother goddess of some kind.

If scholars are unable to tell us exactly *when* religion began, they can however tell us *how* it began.

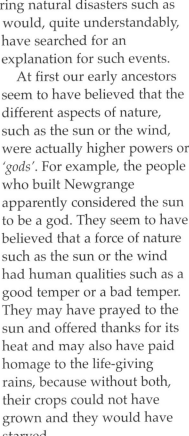

Venus of Willendorf. ➡

How did it begin?

Religion most likely began as an attempt by our early ancestors to explain the workings of the natural world around them. They were puzzled by such things as the weather, the changing of the seasons and the movement of the sun and the moon. They probably found recurring natural disasters such as droughts, floods and storms frightening. They would, quite understandably, have searched for an explanation for such events.

At first our early ancestors seem to have believed that the different aspects of nature, such as the sun or the wind, were actually higher powers or *'gods'*. For example, the people who built Newgrange apparently considered the sun to be a god. They seem to have believed that a force of nature such as the sun or the wind had human qualities such as a good temper or a bad temper. They may have prayed to the sun and offered thanks for its heat and may also have paid homage to the life-giving rains, because without both, their crops could not have grown and they would have starved.

Light illuminating passage and chamber at Newgrange.

Ancient people offering sacrifices to their Gods. ➡

Later, however, our ancestors stopped believing that the sun, the wind and the rain were gods. They came to believe that, *behind* the sun and the wind, there were unseen gods who *controlled* these forces of nature. These gods lived in an invisible world that was *beyond* our natural world. This is why the gods were called *supernatural* beings.

These early religious believers were most likely *polytheists* (i.e. they believed in many gods). They gathered as a community to offer *sacrifices* (i.e. give up something of value) out of love or fear of their gods. They did this in the hope that, if they showed the gods how much they respected them, then the gods would treat them well. They believed that, if there was a good harvest, it was because their gods were happy with their sacrifices and were generous to them in return.

In time, some people came to believe in one God only, while others continued to believe in many gods. Eventually, five major religions emerged:

■ Hinduism,   ■ Judaism,   ■ Buddhism,   ■ Christianity and   ■ Islam.

QUESTIONS

1. What evidence is there that our early ancestors believed in life after death?
2. What did our early ancestors believe about the different aspects of nature, such as the sun or the wind?
3. Why would the people who built Newgrange have thought it necessary to worship the sun?
4. Why did our ancestors later begin to call their gods *supernatural beings*?
5. (a) What does it mean to offer a *sacrifice*?
   (b) Why did ancient peoples offer sacrifices to their gods?

The Blind Men and the Elephant

Consider the story of the six blind men who were asked to describe an elephant by what they felt when they touched one.

'It was six men of Hindustan,
to learning much inclined,
Who went to see the elephant
(though all of them were blind)
That each by observation
Might satisfy his mind.

The First approached the elephant
And, happening to fall
Against his broad and sturdy side,
At once began to bawl:
"I clearly see the elephant
Is very like a wall."

The Second, feeling round the tusk,
Cried: "Ho, what have we here,
So very round and smooth and sharp?
To me, 'tis mighty clear
This wonder of an elephant
Is very like a spear."

The Third approached the animal,
And, happening to take
The squirming trunk within his hand
Thus boldly up and spake;
"I see," quoth he, "the elephant
Is very like a snake."

The Fourth reached out his eager hand
and felt about the knee,
"What most this wondrous beast is like
is mighty plain" said he,
"'Tis clear enough, the elephant
Is very like a tree."

The Fifth, who chanced to touch the ear,
Said "E'en the blindest man
Can tell what this resembles most;
Deny the fact who can
This marvel of an elephant
Is very like a fan."

The Sixth no sooner had begun
About the beast to grope,
Than, seizing on the swinging tail
that fell within his scope,
"I see," quoth he, "The elephant
Is very like a rope."

And so these men of Hindustan
Disputed loud and long
Each in his own opinion
Exceeding stiff and strong,
Though each was partly in the right,
and all were in the wrong.'

(The Blind Men and the Elephant
by John Saxe)

If left on our own, human beings would know very little about God. We would, perhaps, be no closer to understanding God than the six blind men of the story were to describing an elephant. However, the sacred scriptures of the different world religions contain many insights into who God is and what God expects from human beings. How is this so?

Revelation

▲ Abraham is welcomed by a friendly ruler.

Human beings did not discover important truths about God by their own efforts. Rather, at moments in history, God called out to certain special people and *gave* them important insights into who God is and what God wants of human beings. Indeed, the word *God* is thought to have originally meant *a call*.

If we study the stories of the founders of the different religions, we can see how the experience of God calling to them had a tremendous impact on their lives. If we consider the story of Abraham, for example, we can see that Abraham trusted in God so much that he left his homeland and followed God's call to *'go to a land which I will show you'* (*Genesis* 12:1).

All the major religions were founded by individuals who, each in their own way, responded to God's call. Through them God revealed things that human beings could never otherwise have known. For example:

- God is completely good.
- God loves each and every human being.

The gift of such insights into the mystery of God and how people can find true and lasting happiness is called God's *revelation*.

QUESTIONS

1. What was the original meaning of the word *God?*
2. What is meant by God's *revelation?*

JOURNAL WORK

Imagine you are a newspaper reporter. Write an article about what you consider to be the most important aspects of religion. The article should be about two hundred words long.

CHAPTER FOUR

THE DIFFERENT PATHS TO GOD

Introduction

This book is about religion. But religion can only be understood and appreciated when we study the different religions and reflect on their teachings.

The major religions in order of their historical emergence are:

Hinduism	2000 B.C.
Judaism	1850 B.C.
Buddhism	500 B.C.
Christianity	4 B.C.
Islam	A.D. 622

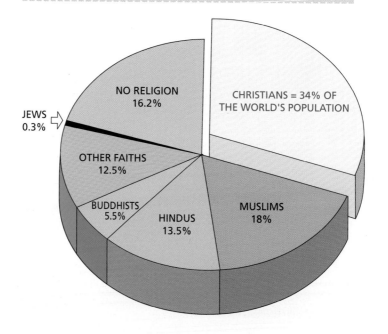

NO RELIGION
16.2%

JEWS
0.3%

OTHER FAITHS
12.5%

CHRISTIANS = 34% OF
THE WORLD'S POPULATION

BUDDHISTS
5.5%

HINDUS
13.5%

MUSLIMS
18%

Different Paths

Each of the major religions offers its *own* set of answers to life's great mysteries. Each has its own separate identity and its own *unique approach* to God.

For example, Hindus worship a variety of gods. Yet, consider the following statements from three other religions:

- *Hear O Israel, the Lord Our God, the Lord is One* Judaism
- *We believe in One God* Christianity
- *There is no God but Allah* Islam

Three major religions – Judaism, Christianity and Islam – believe that there is only *one* God. However, each of them understands God in their *own* way.

Yet, while recognising the fact that there are *many differences* between the major religions, we can also see that they do agree on certain matters.

The Golden Rule

If one reads the sacred scriptures (i.e. holy books) of the different religions, one will notice that they all agree on what is called the *Golden Rule.*

Hinduism
'This is the sum of duty: do nothing to others which would cause you pain if done to you' [Mahabharata 5,1517]

Judaism
'What is harmful to you, do not to your fellow men' [Talmud, Shabbat, 3id]

Buddhism
'Hurt not others in ways that you yourself would find hurtful' [Udana-Varga 5,18]

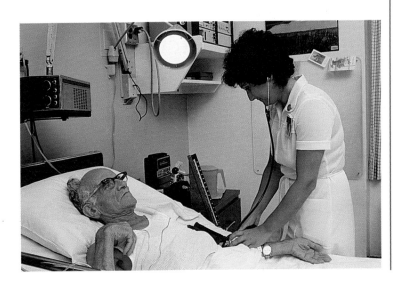

Christianity

'In everything do to others as you would have them do to you' [*Matthew* 7:12]

Islam

'No one of you is a believer until he desires for his brother that which he desires for himself' [*Sunnah*]

Although each of the major religions words this *Golden Rule* differently, they all offer the same guidance. They *all* recommend it as the correct way for people to behave towards one another.

QUESTIONS

1. Re-arrange the following religions in order of their historical emergence and match them with the correct date.

Christianity	500 B.C.
Buddhism	2000 B.C.
Judaism	A.D. 622
Islam	1850 B.C.
Hinduism	4 B.C.

2. Name the religion which encourages the worship of many gods?
3. Which major world religions worship *one* God only?
4. (a) What is the *Golden Rule?* Choose any version of it.
   (b) Why is it important?

Common Characteristics

Generally speaking, all religions have five characteristics in common. They are:

■ Creed   ■ Code   ■ Scripture   ■ Community   ■ Ritual

1. Creed

The word *creed* comes from the Latin word *credo* meaning *I believe*. We may define a creed as:

a shared set of beliefs about God and the meaning of life.

Some religions offer their members a *fixed formula* of what they teach, which may be expressed in the form of a prayer. While these prayers do *not* contain all the teachings of a religion, they do contain its most *important* ones.

For example:

■ All Muslims are expected to recite the same brief creed called the *Shahadah*, which states:

> *'There is no God but God and Muhammad is his prophet.'*

■ The earliest Christian creed is known as the *Apostle's Creed*. It was so called because at one time it was thought to have been set down by the Twelve Apostles themselves. In fact, this creed dates from the third century A.D. It was drawn up and agreed upon after lengthy discussions by a church *council* (i.e. a general meeting of Christian leaders). It was originally used as a clear statement of basic Christian belief for new members of the Christian religion.

Later, in the fourth century A.D., a longer and more detailed creed was composed. This was written to settle disputes between Christians over what they should believe about God. It has been known since as the *Nicene Creed*. Catholics recite it each Sunday during Mass.

▲ Jesus teaching his disciples.

The Apostle's Creed

I believe in God, the Father almighty, creator of heaven and earth.

I believe in Jesus Christ, his only Son, our Lord. He was conceived by the power of the Holy Spirit and born of the Virgin Mary. He suffered under Pontius Pilate, was crucified, died and was buried. He descended to the dead. On the third day he rose again. He ascended into heaven and is seated at the right hand of the Father. He will come again to judge the living and the dead.

I believe in the Holy Spirit, the Holy Catholic Church, the communion of saints, the forgiveness of sins, the resurrection of the body, and the life everlasting. Amen.

The Nicene Creed

We believe in one God, the Father, the almighty, maker of heaven and earth, of all that is, seen and unseen.

We believe in one Lord, Jesus Christ, the only Son of God, eternally begotten of the Father, God from God, Light from Light, true God from true God, begotten, not made, of one Being with the Father. Through him all things were made. For us and for our salvation, he came down from heaven; by the power of the Holy Spirit he became incarnate of the Virgin Mary, and became man. For our sake he was crucified under Pontius Pilate; he suffered death and was buried. On the third day he rose again in accordance with the Scriptures; he ascended into heaven and is seated at the right hand of the Father. He will come again in glory to judge the living and the dead and his kingdom will have no end.

We believe in the Holy Spirit, the Lord, the giver of life, who proceeds from the Father and the Son. With the Father and the Son he is worshipped and glorified. He has spoken through the prophets. We believe in one holy catholic and apostolic church. We acknowledge one baptism for the forgiveness of sins. We look for the resurrection of the dead, and the life of the world to come. Amen.

We shall examine the *Apostle's Creed* in more detail later.

■ In contrast to both Christianity and Islam, Hinduism does *not* offer a single prayer which sums up its beliefs. However, as we shall see in Chapter 19, those who identify themselves as Hindus do *share* the same broad set of beliefs.

The advantages to having a set creed, however, are:

a) It preserves the true *doctrine* (i.e. teaching) of a particular religion.

b) It helps to prevent the spread of *heresy* (i.e. false teachings).

c) It can be learned by heart and easily *memorised*, giving people a clear statement of the basic teachings of their religion.

> **N.B.**
> People who belong to a particular religion, such as Christianity, claim that it is their faith in God and acceptance of their religion's teachings that gives them the strength to face life's challenges each day.

QUESTIONS

1. State the five characteristics common to *all* religions.
2. Explain the meaning of the word *creed*.
3. State the title of the *earliest* Christian creed. When was it composed?
4. What is the name given to the *longer* and *more detailed* Christian creed? When was it drawn up?
5. What are the advantages to a religion in having a set creed?

JOURNAL WORK

Select what is for you a central statement in the Apostle's Creed and, in a paragraph, say what it means for you.

2. Code

Each major world religion offers its members a *code* (i.e. *a set of guidelines for living*), by which they can tell what is right from what is wrong.

As we have already seen, all the major world religions agree upon the *Golden Rule*. However, each offers more detailed guidance for living a good life. For example: Judaism, Christianity and Islam teach that people must try to put the Ten Commandments into practice in their daily lives.

THE TEN COMMANDMENTS

1. I am the Lord your God. Do not worship anyone but me.
2. You must not use the name of the Lord your God in vain.
3. Remember to observe the Sabbath as a holy day.
4. Honour your father and your mother.
5. You must not commit murder.
6. You must not commit adultery.
7. You must not steal.
8. You must not tell lies.
9. You must not covet your neighbour's wife.
10. You must not covet your neighbour's property.

Moses receives the Tablets from the Lord. ➡

These three major world religions teach that people should try to live according to *God's* standards. They believe that only by doing so can people find real and lasting happiness.

3. Scriptures

The scriptures (i.e. holy books) of a particular religion usually contain important stories and key teachings of that religion. These stories and teachings have been recorded to ensure that they are accurately handed down from one generation to the next.

RELIGION	SCRIPTURES
Hinduism	*The Vedas*
Judaism	*The Tenakh* (Hebrew Scriptures)
Buddhism	*The Pali Canon*
Christianity	*The Bible* [Old Testament and New Testament]
Islam	*The Qur'an*

◄ An illuminated page from St Mark's Gospel, Book of Kells.

QUESTIONS

1. Why does each religion offer its members a *code*?
2. Which code is common to Jews, Christians and Muslims?
3. (a) Why were the scriptures of the different religions written?
   (b) What do they contain?
4. Match the correct set of scriptures with its religion.

Hinduism	The Tenakh
Judaism	The Qur'an
Buddhism	The Bible
Christianity	The Vedas
Islam	The Pali Canon

4. Community

Many people who believe in God say that they belong to *two families*. One is their natural family composed of the people to whom they are related: father, mother, brothers, sisters and so on. The other is a much bigger family of all those people who belong to their *religion*, i.e. share the same beliefs.

All religions try to encourage this sense of belonging to a community or family of people. Such a *community of faith* is united by the belief that certain things, such as human life and the world we all share, are *sacred* (i.e. *they inspire total respect)*. Further, this community should offer people the care and support they need when faced with tragedies such as the loss of a loved one.

5. Ritual

Each of the major religions has places specially set aside for its members to gather together to worship their God or gods. For example:

Christians worship in *churches*, Jews in *synagogues* and Muslims in *mosques*. There they conduct or take part in *rituals* (i.e. *religious ceremonies)*. They do so for the following reasons:

■ To *communicate* important teachings about God and the meaning of life.

■ To *encourage* people to remain faithful to God and to keep trying to live according to the teachings of their religion.

The Last Supper. ➡

- To *mark* important moments in their lives. For example, happy occasions such as welcoming the arrival of a new born baby into a local religious community, or a sad occasion such as a funeral.
- To *recall* the important events that brought their religion into being and to tell the story of its founder.
- To *remind* people that as a community of faith, they show their love of God by treating each other with kindness and respect.

These *public* rituals are generally led by religious leaders, such as *priests* for Catholics, or *rabbis* for Jews.

← A Catholic priest.

▼ A Jewish rabbi.

However, rituals can also be *private* and *personal* acts of worship by a believer. For example, a believer may set aside time each day where he/she prays alone to God. This could be something as simple as starting or ending one's day with a prayer.

QUESTIONS

1. Explain the meaning of the following statement:
   Many people who believe in God say that they belong to two families.
2. Identify one thing that *unites* a religious community.
3. Explain the word *ritual*.
4. Why do the members of a religion conduct or take part in rituals?
5. Give an example of a *private* ritual.

Founders

All of the major world religions can trace their origins back to remarkably small and fragile beginnings. Unfortunately, the name of Hinduism's founder(s) has been lost with the passage of time. However, the other four major world religions can trace their beginnings back to one extraordinary founding figure in each case.

Judaism	Abraham
Buddhism	Gautama
Christianity	Jesus
Islam	Muhammad

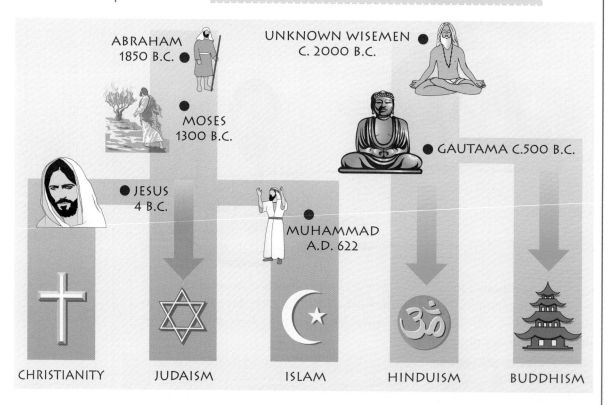

In each case, these founders gathered around them a tiny band of devout followers who carried on their work. In time, their numbers increased until, like tiny acorns, these religions sprouted from their humble beginnings into mighty oak trees. These five major world religions – Hinduism, Judaism, Buddhism, Christianity and Islam – have provided guidance and hope for countless millions of people down through the centuries.

Today, they exert a great influence over the lives of the overwhelming majority of the human race.

Conflict

The five major world religions – Hinduism, Judaism, Buddhism, Christianity and Islam – have certain things in common. That is why each of them is called a *religion*. However, each of these religions has its own unique identity and particular set of teachings about God and the meaning of life.

The differences between the major religions have sadly been a source of conflict over the centuries. Newspapers and television reports often mention how religious disagreements can lead to confrontations such as those between groups of Hindus and Muslims in India or between groups of Christians, Jews and Muslims in Palestine, for the control of places each considers holy.

But too often the headline writers fail to look closely enough at the story. They fail to see that religion is only *one* element of the conflict. Other sources of conflict are quite frequently *overlooked.* For example:

- poverty
- unemployment
- disputes over land ownership
- lack of education
- ethnic or tribal hatred.

Usually religious difference is simply one more ingredient thrown into a mixture of unresolved disputes laced with fear and suspicion. The result can be a time bomb that leads to

▲
Conflict between Hindus and Muslims at Ayodhya, India, 1990.

death and destruction if set off. Consider the horrors of Bosnia, Kosovo, Rwanda or indeed, Northern Ireland, in recent times.

The great Hindu holy man, Mohandas Gandhi (known as Mahatma), was once asked if he believed religion was to blame for some of the terrible crimes committed in history, such as the Nazi Holocaust. Gandhi responded by explaining how the essence of religion was to do *good*, to help people and *not* to harm them. He said that wicked people had *abused* religion, had inflicted great harm and cynically tried to justify it by saying that they were only 'doing God's will'. He ended with this remark:

'The terrible crimes of history are the fault not of religion but of the ungovernable brute in human beings.'

Gandhi and martyrs march to Jalalpur, 1930. ➡

QUESTIONS

1. Match the name of the person in column *B* with the religion he founded in column *A*.

A RELIGION	B NAME
Buddhism	Jesus
Judaism	Gautama
Christianity	Muhammad
Islam	Abraham

2. List six sources of conflict between people in today's world.
3. Read Mohandas Gandhi's comment on where the responsibility for history's great crimes lies.
   (a) Why did he reach this conclusion?
   (b) Do you agree or disagree?
   Give reasons for your answer.

Part Two

Exploring the Mystery of God

CHAPTER FIVE

REASONS FOR BELIEVING

Three Views

Thinking about God is perhaps the most challenging activity that can occupy our minds. The most basic question we have to deal with is – does God really exist?

There are three possible answers to this question

■ *Theism*　　■ *Atheism*　　■ *Agnosticism*

▲
God: the greatest mystery.

DOES GOD EXIST?

THEISM   *Yes* – There is a God.

ATHEISM   *No* – There is no God.

AGNOSTICISM   *Don't know* – It is impossible for human beings to answer this question.

Objections

Most human beings believe that there is a God of some kind. They do so, initially, because they are brought up to believe it. But when they become adults, many *choose* to believe it because they are convinced that it is true.

Some people sincerely doubt that there is a God. They may remark:

How can I be asked to believe in something I cannot see?

This is an understandable reaction. But religion *depends* on the belief that there is far more to life than meets the eye. Religion claims that, *beyond* the natural world which can be observed, measured and explained, there exists an invisible, *super*natural being who knows the answers to life's mysteries. This being is called *God*.

Judaism, Christianity and Islam teach that people should not expect to see God, at least, *not directly*. They do so for two reasons:

1 They believe that God is a *mystery*.

They teach that it is simply beyond our human capacity to ever fully know and understand God.

God is not like a crossword puzzle which can be figured out and then filed away marked '*solved*'.

People can only gradually grow in their knowledge and understanding of God by devoting their lives to prayer, study and doing good deeds.

2 They believe that God is *unique*.

God is not like anything else in human experience.

God is a *pure spirit*, i.e. God does not have a physical body.

Therefore, God *cannot* be directly seen or touched.

Reasons for Believing

What reasons do people have for believing that there is a God?

There is no direct, visible and straightforward evidence that there is a God. However, religious thinkers like Thomas Aquinas have argued that there is *indirect* evidence of this. They argue that, if we look closely at the world around us, we can find this indirect evidence. It points to God's invisible presence behind all things.

We will now consider three examples of this evidence.

▲
St Thomas Aquinas.

A 'Things do not just happen'

Experience shows us that things do *not* 'just happen'. An event does not happen of its own accord – it is *caused* by someone or something.

For example, suppose you walk into an empty room on a dark, winter's evening. There is an electric light already shining in the room. Either *someone* or *something* (e.g. a timer) has switched on the light before you arrived. It did *not* switch itself on. Someone or something had to *cause* the light to turn on.

Many scientists believe that the universe itself began with a vast cosmic explosion which they call *the Big Bang*. Many religious people believe that this did not simply happen of its own accord. They believe that God made the Big Bang happen and *created* the universe in which human beings eventually appeared. The creation of the universe can only be explained by saying that it was *caused* by a *creator*. This being we call *God*.

B 'Someone had to design this. It could not have happened this way by chance'

It is not unusual for people to stop occasionally to admire the beauty of the world: the colours of a sunset, the sound of birdsong or the scent of a flower. But if you examine the petal of any flower, you will see that it is vastly complex, made up of billions of atoms, so tiny that they cannot be seen by the naked eye.

Again, consider how a new-born baby develops gradually over nine months from a tiny, microscopic, fertilised egg.

These everyday wonders do not just develop this way over millions of years, by chance, they are *designed*.

If there is evidence of design involved in something, then there must be a *designer*. This being we call *God*.

C From where do human beings get their sense of right and wrong?

The sense of right and wrong is found in all people, whether they are the Aborigines of the Australian outback or the Inuits of the Canadian Arctic. It speaks to astronauts orbiting the Earth, as well as to doctors treating their patients. This inner voice is not limited to any particular time, place or race of people. It is a *universal* thing. Even the most hardened individuals have been known to be so tortured by the realisation of the harm they have done to others that they have confessed their crimes rather than continue to experience their anguish and guilt. For example there is the case of the group of Japanese war veterans who publicly confessed to atrocities they had

committed against civilians in China in the Second World War. (Reported in: *The Irish Independent*, 14 August 1997).

Human beings are the only creatures on Earth with an awareness of right and wrong and the freedom to choose between them. From where did this come? Why should human beings have it?

Religious thinkers claim that it has been given to human beings by *God.*

QUESTIONS

1. Explain the following terms:

   ■ Theism   ■ Atheism   ■ Agnosticism.
2. On what belief does religion depend?
3. What is meant by each of the following statements:
   a. God is a *supernatural* being.
   b. God is a *mystery*.
   c. God is a *pure spirit*.
4. Why do so many people believe that:
   (a) *God is the creator of the universe*
   (b) *God is the designer of all life*
   (c) *God is the source of our sense of right and wrong.*

JOURNAL WORK

Do you think that the evidence supports those who believe in God or those who do not believe in God? Explain your answer.

Believing *in* and believing *that*

There is an important distinction we must now make between believing *in* something and believing *that* something is the case.

For example, a man believes *that* the World Trade Centre is the tallest building in New York. He has never been to New York. He believes this because he has read it in a book or was told it by someone he trusts.

But believing *that* the World Trade Centre is the tallest building in New York really makes absolutely *no difference* to his life. It is just an interesting fact he has stored away. Perhaps he will use it to answer a quiz question one day.

◄ The World Trade Centre, New York.

Similarly, believing *that* there is a God can mean just as little to a person's daily life. It can be just another piece of information a person files away in the back of his/her mind.

But religion does *not* simply ask people to believe *that* there is a God. Rather, religion asks people to believe *in* God.

Christianity teaches that God is a *person* with whom human beings can have a loving relationship. Experience teaches us that no really strong relationship can exist, unless those involved are prepared to believe *in* each other.

To believe *in* someone means to have *faith in* him/her. To put your trust in him/her and then *act* on it.

As with so many things in life, this is easier to talk about than to do.

Consider the story of the man who was hanging dangerously from a cliff edge, his fingers losing their grip as each second ticked by. '*Is there anyone there?*' he shouted. From far below he heard a voice reply, '*I am here. Let go and I will catch you in my arms.*' After a few seconds the man shouted again. '*Is there anybody else there?*'

Believing *in* God and following the teaching of one's religion is *demanding*. It can be very difficult to continue to believe in God when things go wrong in life. But a *faith-filled* person believes that God is there to guide and strengthen him/her through all of life's turmoil.

QUESTIONS

1. Explain the difference between believing *that* something is the case and believing *in* something.
2. Read the story of the man hanging from the cliff edge once more. What point do you think that it is making about belief/faith *in* God?
3. What is meant by a *faith-filled* person?

The Japanese Martyrs

Over the centuries, different governments have made ruthless attempts to wipe out religion. Read the following story of one such attempt. Then answer the questions below it.

'The story of the Christian community in Japan has been an amazing saga of heroism since the gospel was first preached there by Francis Xavier in 1549. For nearly a century the Catholic Church grew rapidly and spread throughout Japan. But in 1638 the Shogun Hideyoshi, ruler of Japan, decided to exterminate Christians. He believed that Christians put their faith in God before their loyalty to him. This he would not tolerate. When finally the Christians rebelled against his harsh rule, thirty-five *thousand of them were massacred. Some of the victims were subjected to the intolerable torture of the pit: hung upside down, suspended in a hole in the ground and kept in agony for days by torturers who bled them slowly from their temples. This persecution continued until finally all signs of Christianity were obliterated. Japan was then sealed off from all foreign contacts for two centuries.*

The signing of a treaty with the United States in 1854 finally reopened Japan to foreigners. A group of French clergy were allowed open a small chapel in the city of Nagasaki.

One day a remarkable thing happened: a small group of Japanese visited the little mission chapel. One of the priests welcomed them and began talking with them. What he learned amazed him. These Japanese were devout Christians who had secretly managed to hold on to the essentials of the Christian faith for two centuries, although they were without priests and totally isolated from the outside world. There were other groups of these Christians scattered across Japan numbering some ten thousand in all.

When news of this reached the Japanese authorities they reacted with fury, because membership of the Christian religion was still a crime. Many of these brave Christians were cruelly persecuted and killed while others were forced into exile. World opinion stirred up by press reports, however, finally brought an end to the persecution, and in 1889 complete freedom of worship was granted to Christians.'

QUESTIONS

(a) Why did the emperor decide to exterminate Christianity?

(b) When did the persecution stop?

(c) Why was the French priest surprised when he met the Japanese Christians in Nagasaki?

(d) Why did the Japanese authorities finally allow freedom of worship in 1889?

(e) What does this story tell you about the *difference* between someone believing *that* there is a God and believing *in* God?

Christian Belief

Christianity is numerically the world's largest religion. It has members on every continent. An estimated two billion people identify themselves as *Christians*, i.e. followers of Jesus Christ.

The essential beliefs of the Christian religion are expressed in the *Apostles' Creed*. Some *differences* have emerged among Christians, however, as to precisely how these beliefs should be understood.

The Apostles' Creed

The Apostles' Creed has been printed below in eight statements of belief. They are the central statements of the Christian faith.

THE APOSTLES' CREED

1. I believe in God, the Father almighty, creator of heaven and earth.

2. I believe in Jesus Christ, his only Son, our Lord. He was conceived by the power of the Holy Spirit and born of the Virgin Mary.

3. He suffered under Pontius Pilate, was crucified, died and was buried. He descended to the dead. On the third day he rose again. He ascended into heaven.

4. And is seated at the right hand of the Father. He will come again to judge the living and the dead.

5. I believe in the Holy Spirit,

6. the holy catholic church,

7. the communion of saints,

8. the forgiveness of sins, the resurrection of the body and the life everlasting.

Amen.

---

1. **God**

The creed begins with *I believe in God*. This means that Christians believe in *one God only*. They believe that God is *infinite* (i.e. unlimited), *eternal* (i.e. everlasting) and *creator* of the world. This belief that there is one God only is called *monotheism*.

Christians believe that there are *three persons in the one God*: God the *Father*, God the *Son* and God the *Holy Spirit*.

The way in which God is three persons and yet one God is a great *mystery*. This mystery is called the holy (or blessed) *Trinity*.

We shall explore it in detail in a later chapter.

2. **Jesus Christ – The Incarnation**
    Christians believe that Jesus Christ is truly human and truly divine.
    They say that he is the Son of Mary by the power of the Holy Spirit.
    The teaching that Jesus was born of a virgin mother is important to
    the claim that he is the Son of God.

    The word *Incarnation* comes from a Latin word meaning '*in the
    flesh*'. It means that the Son of God became a human being at a
    definite time in the history of the world.

    This too is a profound mystery. We shall examine it in greater detail
    later.

3. **The Crucifixion, Resurrection and Ascension of Jesus**
    The Gospel accounts of the arrest, trial and crucifixion of Jesus are
    very detailed and the fact that Jesus really suffered and died on the
    cross on Calvary (or Golgotha) is of great importance to the Christian
    faith. The resurrection of Jesus on the third day after his burial is the
    heart of the Christian faith.

    By rising from the dead, Jesus defeated the power of death over the
    human race and he gave the promise of eternal life to *all*. The death of
    Jesus who was without sin also obtained forgiveness for the sins of all
    humankind. The ascension of Jesus means that he returned to be with
    God the Father, and only after his personal return to heaven did he
    fulfil his promise of sending the Holy Spirit.

4. **The Judgment**
    In parables like *the sheep and the goats* (*Matthew* 25:31-46) Jesus spoke
    about people being judged at the end of their lives or at the end of the
    world. The parables make it clear that all people will have to account
    for the way in which they have lived their own lives. The three areas
    of their lives which will be judged are:

    ■ **how people have loved God**

    ■ **how they have developed the talents God has given them**

    ■ **how they have loved other people**

    At the judgment God will decide whether a person is worthy of
    eternal life or whether he/she has chosen to live apart from God
    forever. Christians believe that, if they live according to the life and
    example of Jesus Christ himself, their judgment will be a joyful
    occasion and they will share eternal life with God.

5. **The Holy Spirit**

   After Jesus' ascension into heaven, the Holy Spirit came on Pentecost day into the hearts and minds of the apostles. They were strengthened in their faith that Jesus had risen from the dead, and they were able to preach to the people in a new and powerful way. Christians today believe that they too can receive the gift of the Holy Spirit and so have the strength to follow Jesus in their daily lives.

6. The Holy Catholic Church

   Most Christians will say the Apostles' Creed which contains this phrase, but they will not all understand these words in the same way. The word *church* here does not refer to a building used for public Christian worship. Rather, it means what it meant in *New Testament* times – a community of all the people who believe in Jesus Christ and follow his way. The church is the people of God.

   The word '*catholic*' means '*worldwide*'. People in the Protestant tradition mean '*I believe in the holy worldwide community of those who follow Jesus Christ*'. The Catholic tradition, on the other hand, has a different interpretation. Catholics will agree that the church means all the people of God who are led by Jesus Christ. They will also say that Jesus appointed a visible leader of his church on Earth, Peter the Apostle. All those who have followed in this position of authority since Peter, are the *popes* of the Catholic Church. Catholics look to the pope for leadership and guidance.

7. The Communion of Saints

   In the *New Testament*, it is clear that the word 'saints' refers to those who follow Jesus Christ. Paul addressed his letters to '*The Saints who are also faithful in Jesus Christ*'. (*Ephesians* 1:1) By 'the Saints', Paul meant those groups of Christians to whom he was writing. Christians generally mean by the phrase *communion of saints* a fellowship of all those, living or dead, who have believed in Jesus Christ and followed his way of life.

8. **The forgiveness of sins**

The resurrection of the body

Life everlasting

These three promises of the Christian faith are fundamental for anyone who says that he/she is a Christian. Forgiveness of sins in the Christian religion also involves the forgiveness of others.

Christians believe in the bodily resurrection of Jesus based on the *New Testament* accounts of his appearances to his disciples when he ate and drank with them and showed them his wounds.

Christians believe in their own personal resurrection after death because of the promises made by Jesus himself. By everlasting life Christians mean that they believe they will be happy with God for ever if they have lived according to the way shown to them by Jesus Christ.

QUESTIONS

1. Fill in the missing words in the spaces below.
   The Apostles' Creed
   I believe in _____, the Father _____, creator of _____ and _____.
   I believe in Jesus Christ, his ____ _____, our Lord. He was _____by the power of the ___ _____ and born of the ___ ____.

   He suffered under ____ _____, was crucified, _____ and was buried. He descended to the _____ .
   On the third day he ____ again. He ____ into heaven and is seated at the ___ ____ of the Father. He will come again to _____the living and the dead.
   I believe in the Holy Spirit, the holy _____ _____, the communion of _____, the _____ of sins, the _____ of the body and the life _____.

2. What do Christians believe about the Holy Spirit's role in their lives?
3. What point is Jesus making in the Parable of the Sheep and the Goats?
4. What are the two meanings of the word *church*?
5. Explain the different interpretations of the term *catholic* in the phrase *the holy catholic church* given by (a) those in the *Catholic* Christian tradition and (b) those in the *Protestant* Christian tradition.
6. What do Christians mean when they talk about *the communion of saints*?
7. In the Christian religion, what does *the forgiveness of sin* also involve?
8. What do Christians mean when they talk about *everlasting life*?

CHAPTER SIX

GOD IN JUDAISM

The Chosen People

In this chapter, we will examine the Jewish understanding of God. Judaism is the world's oldest monotheistic faith. Its members trace their origins back to *Abraham*, a holy man who lived in the Middle East around 1850 B.C.

The Jewish scriptures tell the story of how God made a *covenant* (i.e. a sacred agreement) with Abraham that his descendants would be God's *chosen people*.

God would do good things for them and through them God would do great things for all the world. They were to offer *example* to other peoples and bring the light of God's love to the whole world.

Moses leading the Exodus.

This covenant was renewed by *Isaac* and *Jacob,* son and grandson of Abraham, and later by the prophet *Moses*.

The people's part in this covenant was to serve God in a spirit of love and total trust. They were to keep God's laws. These laws, known as the *Ten Commandments* were given to Moses, as he led the Jewish people out of captivity in Egypt.

Judaism was the *first* of the major world religions to emphasise that religion is *more* than a matter of performing special ceremonies to worship God. They realised that people show their love for God by treating each other with honesty, kindness and respect.

The Jews established an independent kingdom and, for a time, they prospered. They were ruled by a series of kings, the most important of whom were *David* and *Solomon*. However, the people often forgot their covenant with God and fell into wicked ways. So God sent *prophets* to remind them to keep their promises.

Unfortunately the Jewish nation split into two rival kingdoms. Each was easily conquered by more powerful neighbours. The Jewish people endured great suffering. The Temple of Solomon was destroyed (586 B.C.) and the Jews were exiled to Babylon. There, without the Temple, without a homeland or a king, the Jews learned to depend upon God as their only refuge.

Half a century later, the Jews returned from exile and rebuilt the Temple. But this second temple was destroyed by the Romans following a Jewish uprising in A.D. 70. Then, in A.D. 135, the Jews were forcibly dispersed throughout the world, so beginning what is known as the *Diaspora*.

After many centuries of persecution and upheaval, the greater majority of modern Jews have settled in the state of *Israel*, the land which they believe God promised to Abraham and his descendants. There are also Jewish communities scattered across the globe, most notably in North America and Europe.

QUESTIONS

1. Who was the founder of Judaism?
2. Explain the *covenant* made between God and Abraham.
3. What did God want the people to do in return? How did they do this?
4. Judaism was the first major world religion to emphasise what idea?
5. Why did God send the prophets?
6. What did the Jewish people learn to do in Babylon?
7. What event happened in A.D. 70?
8. What was the *Diaspora*? When did it occur?

Holy Books

The sacred writings of the Jewish religion are divided into three sections:

1 **Torah** – means '*instruction*'. This is also called the *Pentateuch*, from the Greek word for 'five', because it consists of five books: *Genesis, Exodus, Leviticus, Numbers* and *Deuteronomy*. It is considered the holiest part of the Jewish scriptures.

   Orthodox Jews believe that these books were given by God to Moses.

2 **Nevi'im** – contains the writings of the Prophets, namely Amos, Hosea, Isaiah and so on.

3 **Ketuvim** – includes writings such as the *Psalms* and the *Proverbs*.

   The *Psalms* are beautiful poems and songs. According to tradition, most were supposed to have been composed by King David. The *Psalms* use language to express a great range of different emotions – joy, sadness, anger, wonder. But all the *Psalms* speak in loving terms to God whom they praise as the ruler of the universe.

The initial letters of each of the three section headings of the Jewish scriptures – *T N K* – are used to form the word *Tenakh*. This is the name the Jews give to their sacred scriptures. Christians refer to these holy writings as either the *Old Testament* or the *Hebrew Scriptures*.

   The oldest complete manuscript of the *Tenakh* is housed and displayed in the Sanctuary of the Book in Jerusalem. It was discovered near the Dead Sea. It is a marvellous treasure trove of insights into the Jewish understanding of God.

QUESTIONS

1. What does the word *Torah* mean?
2. Why is it sometimes called the *Pentateuch*?
3. What do Orthodox Jews believe about the *Torah*?
4. What are contained in (a) the *Nevi'im* and (b) the *Ketuvim*?
5. Write a brief note on the *Psalms*.
6. Choose any Psalm and write a brief report on what it contains.
7. From where does the name *Tenakh* derive? To what does it refer?
8. Where is the oldest complete manuscript of the *Tenakh* housed and displayed?

The Dead Sea Scrolls

In 1947 some Bedouin Arabs were smuggling goats into southern Israel. As they passed through the desolate Qumran wilderness near the Dead Sea, one of their goats strayed away from the herd.

The cliffs of Qumran.
▼

A young boy was sent to bring the animal back. He had to climb along steep, rocky hillsides to catch up with it. As he passed the opening of a large cave, the boy paused for a moment. He picked up a stone and threw it into the cave's dark interior. To his great surprise he then heard the sound of something breaking. The boy summoned up his courage and went in to explore the cave.

Inside the cave he found a row of tall clay jars. Each jar contained bundles of *manuscripts* (i.e. handwritten documents). These manuscripts were sewn together in long scrolls and wrapped in linen. They are now known as the *Dead Sea Scrolls.*

When these scrolls were carefully unrolled and examined by scholars in Jerusalem, they proved to be a find of enormous importance. The scrolls were discovered to be handwritten copies of the *Tenakh*. They had been hidden in that cave by Jewish scholars some time in the mid-first century A.D. The identity of the people who put them in this hiding place has been a matter of some controversy among scholars. However, they were most likely hidden to prevent their destruction by the Romans.

QUESTIONS

1. Who discovered the *Dead Sea Scrolls?*
2. Where were they discovered?
3. How had they been stored?
4. What was written on the *Dead Sea Scrolls?*
5. When were they hidden?
6. Why were they hidden?

God in the Tenakh

The *Dead Sea Scrolls* tell us a great deal about the religion of the Jewish people in the time of Jesus. The Jews believed that the name of God was *Yahweh*. However, they considered God's name to be so holy that they agreed that it should *never* be either spoken or written. As a result, whenever the authors of the *Dead Sea Scrolls* had to refer to God's name, it was replaced in the manuscript by *four dots*.

These four dots tell us a great deal about how the Jewish authors of the *Tenakh* thought about God. The *Tenakh* teaches that God – *Yahweh* – is holy and loving, but also *awe-inspiring*. Yahweh is a *distant* being. Yahweh only appeared on earth to speak to specially chosen people, who were known as *the prophets*.

We will now consider two examples which illustrate the way in which the authors of the *Tenakh* thought about God.

■ Example One
Read this extract from the account of how God called *Moses* to begin his mission to free the Hebrews from slavery in Egypt.

> *Moses was looking after the flock of Jethro, his father-in-law. He*
> *led his flock to the far side of the wilderness and came to Horeb,*
> *the mountain of God. Moses looked; there was the bush blazing*
> *but it was not being burnt up. 'I must go and look at this strange*
> *sight,' Moses said 'and see why the bush is not burnt.'*
> *Yahweh called to him from the middle of the bush.*
> *'Moses, Moses,' he said.*
> *'Here I am,' Moses answered.*

'Come no nearer,' Yahweh said. 'Take off your
shoes for the place on which you stand is holy
ground. I am the God of your father, the God
of Abraham, the God of Isaac, and the God
of Jacob.'
At this Moses covered his face, afraid to look
at God.
[Exodus 3:1-6]

Moses before the Burning Bush
by Raphael.

■ Example Two

Read this extract from the vision of Yahweh's glory and majesty given to
Isaiah while he was praying in the Temple in Jerusalem.

*In the year of King Uzziah's death, I saw the
Lord Yahweh seated on a high throne. Above
him stood angels.
And they cried out to one another in this way.
    Holy, holy, holy is Yahweh
    His glory fills the whole earth.
The foundations of the threshold shook with
the voice of the one who cried out, and the
temple was filled with smoke.*
[Isaiah 6:1-5]

Isaiah by Gustav Dore.

GOD IN THE TENAKH

God was revealed through the prophets to be

- *a pure spirit* (i.e. a being who does not have a physical body)
- *a person* (i.e. someone with whom people can form a relationship)
- *faithful* (i.e. worthy of people's trust)
- *perfect* (i.e. completely good)
- *merciful* (i.e. one who loves and forgives the repentant sinner)
- *a guide* (i.e. one who offers people love and support in the face of life's challenges)
- *the creator* (i.e. the one who made the universe)
- *universal* (i.e. the God of *all* people)
- *all powerful* (i.e. nothing is beyond God's power)
- *eternal* (i.e. a being who lives *outside* of time, was never born, does not age and will never die).

QUESTIONS

1. What did the Jews believe was God's name?
2. How did the Jews show their respect for God's name?
3. Having read the two extracts from the *Tenakh* above, what evidence do you find in *each* of them to show that the God of Moses and of Isaiah was an *awe-inspiring* and *distant* being.

A Faithful People

The faith of the Jewish people in Yahweh has been tested many times in their long history. Never more so than in the nightmare years of Nazi Germany. Between 1933 and 1945 some six million Jewish people, one-and-a-half million of them children, were systematically murdered in concentration camps.

Yet, even throughout this horrific and terrifying ordeal, a large core of Jewish people kept their faith in God. Despite the vicious treatment they received, they still believed that God cared for them and loved them. They saw their suffering as the work of hate-filled people, *not* God.

▲ Jewish people being rounded up by Nazis to be sent to the concentration camps.

The achievement of the Jewish people is quite extraordinary. As Loretta Pastva has written:

No people, so widely dispersed and as often persecuted as the Jews have been, has ever kept a faith alive for so long.

This is a topic to which we shall return in *Book Three*.

JOURNAL WORK

In your view, what is it about religion that helps people through even the most terrible ordeal?

CHAPTER SEVEN

GOD IN CHRISTIANITY I: THE INCARNATION

Introduction

In Book One, we traced the story of how Christianity sprang forth from Judaism in the first century A.D.

Like the Jews, Christians believe in and worship *one* God only. Both religions teach that God is the Supreme Being, the creator of the universe and awesome beyond compare. Yet, God is also said to love and care for each and every human being.

As we shall see, however, Christians understand this one God in a *different* way to Jews.

Difference

Christians believe that their ideas about God are based on the insights first revealed by God to the Jewish people through the prophets. These revelations were recorded in the Tenakh, which Christians refer to as the *Old Testament* or the Hebrew Scriptures.

However, whereas the *Tenakh* presents God as being at an unbridgeable distance from human beings, Christians think of God very differently. They believe that through his teaching, healing, death and resurrection, Jesus of Nazareth not only *summed up* the *Jewish* understanding of God, but *surpassed* (i.e. went beyond) it.

Christians believe that God is *not* distant. The *New Testament* tells the story of how Jesus of Nazareth *bridged* the wide chasm or distance between God and human beings. Christians claim that God so loved human beings that *in Jesus, God became a human being* and lived among us. As one evangelist put it:

*The Holy Family –
Bartolomé
Murillo.* ➡

The Word became flesh and dwelt among us.
John 1:14.

We will now turn to consider *why* Christians came to believe this.

The Incarnation

From the beginning of Jesus' public ministry, people were asking:

Who is this?
Mark 1:27.

When trying to answer this question, Jesus' followers reflected on all that had happened:

■ Jesus' miracles
■ his preaching about the Kingdom of God

- his trial and death
- his resurrection.

Indeed, they had so much to think about that these early Christians took many years to gradually work out what it all meant. The more they prayed, discussed and reflected on what they had experienced, the more they realised how *extraordinary* were the conclusions they reached.

1. They accepted Jesus as God's special 'anointed one' – the *Messiah* or *Christ* – whom the prophets had said God would send. But they believed that Jesus was also *much more*.

2. These first Christians carefully considered how Jesus *himself* understood his relationship to God:

   - According to the *New Testament*, at Jesus' baptism, a voice from heaven declared

   > *You are my Son, whom I love, with you I am well pleased.*
   > *Luke* 3:22.

- Jesus constantly referred to God as *My Father* (see for example: *Luke* 10:22 or *Matthew* 10:32-33).

- Jesus shocked his fellow Jews by referring to God as *Abba,* a word Jewish children used when addressing their fathers. A modern equivalent would be 'Daddy' (see *Luke* 11:2 and 9-13). The Jewish authorities of the time considered such a way of speaking about God to be disrespectful.

- Jesus emphasised that because of this special Father/Son relationship, he was now the *supreme channel of communication* between God and human beings. (see *John* 14:6).

- Furthermore, in Jewish thinking, a father is seen in his son. When Jesus called God *my Father*, he was saying that people could see what God is like through *him*. (see *John* 14: 8-11)

▲
The mosaic inside the Hagia Sophia, Istanbul (Twelfth Century).

Indeed, Jesus is quoted as saying

> *The Father and I are one.*
> *John* 10:25.

The early Christians were confronted with a deep *mystery*. Jesus of Nazareth was a human being:

■ He got tired.

■ He knew what it was to be hungry and thirsty.

■ He experienced the full range of human emotions, from joy to sorrow.

■ He suffered and died on the cross.

But Jesus could do things that *only* God could do. Jesus was a completely *unique* person:

■ He healed those sick in mind or body, instantly.

■ He raised the dead to life.

■ He himself rose from the dead on Easter Sunday. They concluded that *when they saw Jesus, they saw God in human form* (see *Philippians* 2:5-11).

In time, Christians began to refer to Jesus as the *Incarnation* (meaning: *in the flesh*). Christians believe that Jesus of Nazareth is *God made man.*

The Christian *doctrine* (i.e. teaching) of the *Incarnation* is complex and easily misunderstood. It does *not* mean that Jesus is part man and part God. Rather, it means that Jesus is both *fully* human and *fully* divine.

The *Cathecism of the Catholic Church* (no. 464) teaches that *Jesus Christ is true God and true man.*

Importance

The Incarnation means that God is *not* distant. God is *very near* to human beings.

One story that serves to illustrate this is *The Long Silence*, the author of which is unknown. It is set on the Last Day, or as it is sometimes called *Judgment Day.*

In this story, people who have suffered terribly in their lives complain that *God leads a pretty sheltered life.* To qualify as their Judge, they say, God should be sentenced to live on Earth as a human being.

'Let him be born a Jew. Let him be doubted by his family and betrayed by his friends. Let him face false charges and be tried by a prejudiced jury in front of a hostile crowd. Let him be tortured to death – and as he dies, let him feel abandoned and alone.'

When this judgment was pronounced, there was a long silence. Nobody moved. For suddenly all knew that God had already served his sentence.

Christians believe in and worship a God who is very *close* to human beings. That is why Christians have called Jesus *Emmanuel*, meaning *God - with - us.*

↞ *Christ on the Cross* by Rembrandt.

QUESTIONS

1. (a) Explain the meaning of the word *Abba* in the time of Jesus.
   (b) What point was Jesus making when he referred to God in this way?
2. Read the following statements attributed to Jesus:
   (a) *Anyone who has seen me has seen the Father. John* 14:9
   (b) *The Father and I are one. John* 10:25
   What do Christians believe he meant by them?
3. Explain the Christian doctrine of the *Incarnation*. State:
   (a) The meaning of the word itself.
   (b) What it does not mean.
   (c) What it does mean.
4. Why do Christians sometimes refer to Jesus as *Emmanuel*?

JOURNAL WORK

What are the qualities displayed by Jesus that you find most attractive? Perhaps in your answer, you might refer to some of the Gospel stories.

CHAPTER EIGHT

GOD IN CHRISTIANITY II: THE TRINITY

Introduction

Jesus' first followers were devout Jews who uncompromisingly believed that

> *The Lord, Our God, the Lord is One.*
> *Deuteronomy 6:4.*

But their whole understanding of God had been *expanded* and enriched as a result of the time they had shared with Jesus.

They came to believe that Jesus was *the Son of God.* This meant that they attributed to Jesus the same characteristics as God (see *Matthew* 16:15-16 and *John* 20:24-29). This *raised huge questions* for them as Jews.

In their search for answers as to what all this meant for their belief in *one* God, these early Christians reflected carefully on what Jesus had taught them:

- Jesus referred to God as his *Father.* He frequently prayed to the Father and said that he and the Father were *one.*

- Since he would no longer be physically present after his Ascension, Jesus promised that he would send the *Holy Spirit.*
  On Pentecost Sunday, Jesus *did* send the Holy Spirit.

- When Jesus sent his disciples out to spread the Gospel message, he used the words:

> *Go, therefore, and make disciples of all nations; baptising them in*
> *the name of the Father and of the Son and of the Holy Spirit.*
> *Matthew 28:19-20.*

Having been brought up as Jews, these early Christians had a deep appreciation for the mystery of God. They believed that God was *beyond* our human ability to ever completely understand. However, they realised that through Jesus, they had been granted a *great insight* into the God they worshipped.

In their prayers they began to refer to God *the Father*, God *the Son* and God *the Holy Spirit*. For example, Paul ends one of his letters with this blessing:

> *May the grace of the Lord Jesus Christ and the love of God and*
> *the fellowship of the Holy Spirit be with you all.*
> *2 Corinthians* 13:14.

This Christian way of referring to God as *Three Persons* – Father, Son and Spirit – is called *Trinitarian language*.

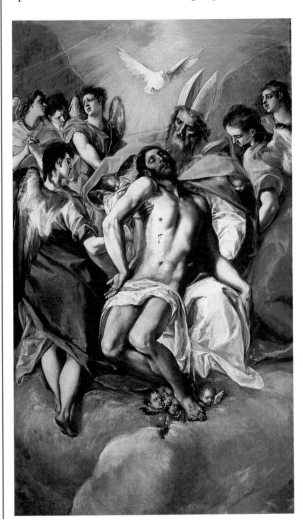

The Holy Trinity is depicted in this sixteenth-century painting by El Greco. The Father is shown holding his crucified Son, with the Holy Spirit hovering as a dove.

The belief that there are *three persons in the one God* is called the doctrine (i.e. teaching) of *the Trinity*.

> **N.B.**
> Although the reasons why Christians accept the doctrine of the Trinity are found in the *New Testament*, the *term* 'Trinity' is not mentioned in it. The *term* itself was not agreed upon until *after* the *New Testament* had been written.

Importance

The doctrine of the Trinity is *central* to all Christian belief and worship. For example, at both the beginning and the end of the Mass, the priest addresses the congregation in a three-fold formula which does not simply refer to *God* but to the Father, the Son and the Holy Spirit.

■ In his opening blessing the priest says:

In the name of the Father and of the Son and of the Holy Spirit.

■ In his concluding blessing the priest says:

May Almighty God bless you, the Father, the Son and the Holy Spirit.

QUESTIONS

1. To what religion did Jesus' first followers belong?
2. What had they been brought up to believe about God?
3. Where do we find evidence that the early Christians prayed to God the Father, God the Son and God the Holy Spirit?
4. What is the Christian doctrine of the *Trinity*?
5. Give an example to show how the doctrine of the Trinity is *central* to all Christian worship?

Exploring the Trinity

The Christian doctrine of the Trinity is complex. It is a profound mystery. Sometimes people think that Christians really believe in three Gods, while claiming to believe in one! *No.* Christians are *monotheists*.

Christians worship *one God only*. But they believe that *there are three distinct persons in one God*. This is called the *triune* or three-in-one God.

Clarification

Christians do *not* believe that
■ one God equals three Gods
or that
■ three Gods equal one God

Christians *do* believe that
■ each of the three persons of the Trinity is *fully* God, *not* one third of God.
■ each member of the Trinity is a separate and distinct person.

Study this diagram carefully. It is taken from a medieval painting. It seeks to help us understand the doctrine of the Trinity.

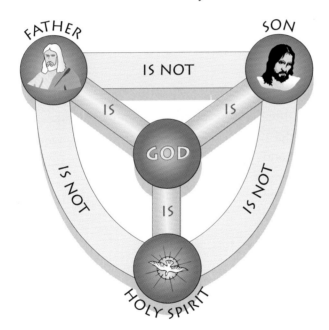

Notice how each member of the Trinity is a distinct person:

The Father is *not* the Son.
The Son is *not* the Father.
The Holy Spirit is *neither* the Father *nor* the Son.
Each is God, yet still there is only *one* God.
How can this be the case?

Over the centuries, Christian thinkers have sought to help people grow in their understanding of the mystery of the Trinity.
Consider the following *two* explanations:

Explanation 1

THE
SON WHO
REVEALS HIMSELF OUT
OF LOVE FOR
HUMAN BEINGS.
JOHN 1:1-14

THE FATHER
WHO CREATES
AND SUSTAINS **GOD**
OUR WORLD. **IS...** THE HOLY
SPIRIT WHO
GENESIS 1-2:4 GIVES LIFE AND
STRENGTH TO
PEOPLE.
ACTS 2:1-4

Each person of the Trinity reflects a particular aspect of God. Each person – Father, Son and Spirit – shows God relating to the world in a different way.

There is the well-known story of how St Patrick used the *shamrock* to help people grow in understanding of the Trinity.

- The shamrock has three leaves but is still *one* plant.

- The Trinity has three persons but there is only *one* God.
- Each person of the Trinity reveals God relating to the world in a different way. Yet it is *one* and the *same* God who does so.

Study the diagram which illustrates each person of the Trinity relating to the world in a different way.

Explanation 2

The early Christians concluded that

God is love.
1 John 4:8.

If God *is* love, then each person of the Trinity must be understood in terms of this love.

One Catholic *theologian* (i.e. religious thinker) has written:

← The Holy Trinity. Here the three triangles are joined into one circle to stand for the idea of the Three Persons in the unity of the One God.

In the Trinity, we get a wonderful understanding of what it means to say God is love. We get a perfect insight into the inner life of God. The three persons in the Holy Trinity are three distinct persons, but they are so in love with each other, so wrapped up in each other, so close to one another, that they are perfectly one. Their communion is so strong, their love so deep that the three become one, while never losing their individuality. God is an eternal (i.e. unending) exchange of infinite (i.e. unlimited) love.

Source: *Sunday Message* [30 May 1999]

QUESTIONS

1. Explain the following statement:
   Christians are monotheists.
2. What does it mean to say that:
   Christians believe in and worship a triune God?
3. Identify which of the following are *true* and which are *false*.
   (a) *The Trinity means that one God equals three Gods.*
   (b) *The Trinity means that each of the three persons is fully God and not one third of God.*
   (c) *The Trinity means that three Gods equal one God.*
4. Fill in the missing details below:
   Each person of the Trinity shows God relating to the world in a different way.

GOD IS

The Father who

_____

_____

_____

The Son who

_____

_____

_____

The Holy Spirit who

_____

_____

_____

5. A Catholic theologian says that *'The relationships in the Trinity are the model for the relationships Christians should have with one another. People should relate to each other as a community of love, unity and harmony.'*

In what way does this statement help people to understand the importance of the Trinity?

Concluding reflection

The doctrine of the Trinity is complex. But the Christians who first set out this doctrine were not primarily concerned with what is understandable. Rather, they were concerned with what is *true*.

Consider the following story. It illustrates the kind of difficulties people face when they try to explain what they mean by the word *God*.

One morning, two great scholars were walking along the coast of North Africa. As they walked they were discussing the meaning of God. Each was convinced that the other was making a poor job of explaining what he understood God to be. Both were able to raise objections to everything the other said.

Suddenly they came upon a small boy playing by the water's edge. He had dug a small pit in the sand and kept running down to the sea, dipping his toy bucket in the water and running back up the beach to empty the water into the pit. They watched for some time as he ran to and fro. They found the scene amusing. They then went up to him and asked what he was doing. The child pointed to the sea and told them, very seriously, that he was going to take all the water in the sea and pour it into the pit he had dug out in the sand.

The two men smiled and then continued on their way. They carried on their discussion. Suddenly one of them stopped. 'You know,' he said, 'we were amused just now when that child told us what he was trying to do. Yet, what we are trying to do in our discussion about God is just the same.'

It is just as impossible for human beings to fully understand God as it was for that child to put all the sea into the little pit he had dug in the sand.

Our minds are as tiny as thimbles. The reality of God is as great as the ocean.

The doctrine of the Trinity, like that of the Incarnation, is a deep *mystery*.

Our human language does not possess words adequate to express it.

Our human minds do not have the capacity to fully understand it.

However, Christians believe that through prayer, good deeds and study, a person may grow in understanding of the mystery of God.

The Prayer of St Patrick
'I bind unto myself today
the strong name of the Trinity
By invocation of the same
the Three in One, and One in Three.
Of whom all nature hath creation,
Eternal Father, Spirit, Word,
Praise to the Lord of our salvation
Salvation is of Christ the Lord.'

JOURNAL WORK

Having reflected on the mystery of the Trinity, what kind of qualities should a truly Christian community have?

In your answer, consider how Christians should treat people in the wider community who are not their relatives and friends.

Part Three

Christianity:
Traditions and Divisions

CHAPTER NINE

ORIGINS

Introduction

Some people find the divisions among Christians puzzling. They are all said to be followers of Jesus Christ. Yet, they belong to different groups, some of whom have actually fought with each other in the past. How did this happen? What are the main differences between them? How are we to understand these divisions within the Christian religion?

Some Christian writers have offered the following approach. They say that we should think of the Christian religion as a *great tree*. The roots of this tree are grounded in the person of Jesus Christ. On two occasions in its history, the trunk of this great tree has *branched off* to produce the three different traditions *within* Christianity today. They are:

■ *Catholicism*   ■ *Orthodoxy*   and   ■ *Protestantism.*

The story of *how* this happened is long and complex. We can only offer the briefest of outlines here.

N.B.
It is important to remember, that the people who belong to these different traditions are *not* members of different religions. On the contrary, they worship the *same* God and *share* certain core beliefs. They are all members of the *one* religion – *Christianity*.

Split Occurs A.D. 1054

THE GREAT SCHISM

The Eastern tradition and the Western tradition had a great deal in common in terms of teaching and worship. However, differences in culture (e.g. language) and disputes over the leadership of the Christian religion grew stronger. Gradually, the two traditions began to move apart. Tragically, they separated from one another in A.D. 1054 in an event referred to as *the Great Schism*. Christianity was thereafter divided into the Catholic Church in the West and the Orthodox Church in the East.

THE DEVELOPMENT OF TWO TRADITIONS

In A.D. 313 the Emperor Constantine made Christianity the official religion of the Roman empire. This decision ended centuries of persecution but had serious long-term consequences for the Christian religion.

In A.D. 320 the capital of the Roman Empire was moved, by Constantine, east to Constantinople (now Istanbul). This led to the development of two sections within Christianity:

■ an Eastern (Greek-speaking) tradition based on Constantinople
and

■ a Western (Latin-speaking) tradition based on Rome.

THE EARLY CHRISTIANS

From its beginnings there were differences within Christianity as to how the *New Testament* should be understood. A series of councils discussed and clarified Christian teaching. Most of the difficulties were resolved by the *Nicene Creed*.

Rooted in Jesus Christ

THE DIVISION OF CHRISTIANITY INTO THREE TRADITIONS

THE ORTHODOX CHURCHES

In the aftermath of the Great Schism, the Orthodox Church came under severe pressure from the expansion of Islam in Asia Minor and North Africa. Although Constantinople itself was conquered by Muslims in 1453, the Orthodox tradition survived. By then it had spread throughout the Balkans and across Russia.

As the Orthodox tradition spread, each country acquired its own independent and self-governing Orthodox Church. The principal ones are:

- Armenian
- Ethiopian
- Greek and
- Russian.

Each is governed by a *patriarch*, the most senior of whom is the Patriarch of Constantinople. However, unlike the Pope in the Catholic Church, he is not the leader of a single united church. Rather, the Patriarch of Constantinople is respected as 'first among equals' and provides leadership at meetings of the different Orthodox Churches. Today, there are about two hundred and fifty million members of the various Orthodox Churches.

EAST AND WEST

ROME, CAPITAL OF THE WESTERN CHURCH

ROME

CONSTANTINOPLE

CONSTANTINOPLE, CAPITAL OF THE EASTERN CHURCH

MEDITERRANEAN SEA

ALEXANDRIA

ANTIOCH

BLACK SEA

THE CATHOLIC CHURCH

Spurred on by the great split in the Church, the Pope called the Council of Trent to begin a process of reform. The Catholic Church over the following centuries underwent a massive expansion in the Americas, Asia and Africa. Today it is the largest of the Christian traditions, with over one billion members worldwide.

Split Occurs A.D. 1517

THE CATHOLIC CHURCH

In the period following the Great Schism, the Catholic Church grew immensely powerful under the leadership of successive popes. The Catholic Church teaches that the popes are the direct successors of the Apostle Peter, to whom Jesus gave a special authority over the whole Christian community (see *Matthew* 16:18-19). However, with great power comes great temptation. Some churchmen abused the power with which they had been entrusted. This led to a strong desire for reform within the Catholic Church. Tragically, this was not acted upon in time.

THE REFORMATION

On 31 October 1517, a Catholic monk named Martin Luther posted 95 theses (i.e. topics for discussion) on the door of Wittenburg Cathedral in Germany. Luther's theses protested against certain corrupt practices, that had developed within the Catholic Church (hence the name *Protestant*).

Soon Luther began to publicly reject important teachings of the Catholic Church concerning the seven sacraments and the authority of the Pope. Finally, Luther was *excommunicated* (i.e. expelled) from the Catholic Church. He established the *Lutheran* Church in Germany.

THE PROTESTANT CHURCHES

Luther's ideas spread rapidly across Europe and eventually to North America. However, Lutheranism was soon only one of many separate Protestant Churches. Indeed, Protestantism quickly revealed a strong tendency to divide into new *denominations* (i.e. separate branches). The chief ones are:

- Lutheran
- Anglican
- Presbyterian
- Baptist
- Methodist
- Quaker

QUESTIONS

1. Identify the *three* main traditions within the Christian religion.
2. (a) What was the *Great Schism*?
   (b) When did it occur?
   (c) Why did it happen?
3. (a) What is a *patriarch*?
   (b) Who is the *most senior* patriarch?
   (c) What authority does he have within the Orthodox tradition?
4. Why did a great desire for reform develop within the Catholic tradition by the early sixteenth century?
5. Explain the origin of the name *Protestant*.
6. What is a *denomination*?
7. Why did the Pope call the Council of Trent?

The Republic of Ireland

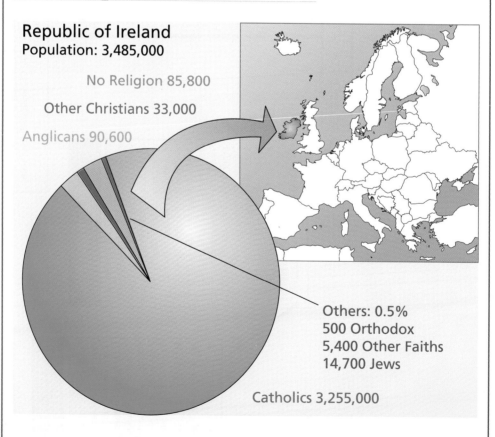

Republic of Ireland
Population: 3,485,000

No Religion 85,800

Other Christians 33,000

Anglicans 90,600

Others: 0.5%
500 Orthodox
5,400 Other Faiths
14,700 Jews

Catholics 3,255,000

The Christian Churches in Ireland

As the diagram shows, the greater majority of Irish people identify themselves as belonging to one or other of the Christian traditions – principally *Catholicism* or *Protestantism*. We shall examine the Catholic Church first, before turning to consider the Protestant Churches.

> **N.B.**
> For Christians, the word 'church' has several meanings:
> 1 an *organisation* (like the Catholic Church or Methodist Church)
> 2 the *people* who are members of the whole worldwide Christian community
> 3 a *building* for worship.

JOURNAL WORK

What does the idea of membership of a particular religion mean to you?

CHAPTER TEN

CATHOLICISM

Introduction

Since the Second Vatican Council (1962-1965), the Catholic Church has emphasised the idea that, although it is organised on a hierarchical basis (i.e. with different levels, one above the other), **all** *baptised people are* **equal** *in their membership and responsibility*. Together they form *one* community of faith referred to as *the people of God*.

Every person has been given certain gifts or talents by God. The Catholic church encourages people to use these gifts in a spirit of generosity and compassion, in whatever role they play, whether it is as a member of the laity or of the clergy.

The Apostolic Succession

The Catholic Church claims that it is the *main trunk* of the Christian family tree. It teaches that it is in *direct continuity* with the first Christian community founded by Jesus Christ himself. Jesus chose the apostles to *continue* his work. The authority of the apostles has been *handed down* from one generation to another over the last two thousand years in what is called the *Apostolic Succession*. A bishop passes this authority on, by laying his hands on the head of a man being made a bishop. As a result, the Catholic bishops claim to be the direct *successors* of the original apostles.

The Pope

Jesus made Peter the leader of the apostles and so gave them *unity* (see *Matthew* 16:18-19). The Pope is the successor to Peter and so, possesses a unique authority.

The Catholic Church is *united* through the power of the Holy Spirit under the leadership of the Pope in Rome. The Pope is called the *Vicar of Christ* (i.e. he is Christ's representative on Earth). The Pope is the visible head of the whole Church and his authority extends to all its members.

The First Vatican Council (1870) declared that, when speaking on the essential matters of the faith, and when certain strict criteria are fulfilled, the Pope is *infallible* (i.e. he cannot err).

The Pope is chosen by *conclave*, (i.e. a secret assembly or meeting of the *cardinals* of the Catholic Church). A cardinal is a member of the select group of bishops who may cast their vote when a new pope is being chosen. Most countries have at least one cardinal.

The Bishops

Within the Catholic Church there are *local churches* called

St Peter's, Rome.

dioceses. Each is led by a *bishop*. It is the role of the bishop to interpret the authoritative teaching of the Church for the people of his diocese.

In most countries, Catholic bishops meet together on a regular basis to discuss important matters. These gatherings are called *Episcopal Conferences*. In Ireland, they usually take place at St Patrick's College, Maynooth, Co Kildare.

The Catholic bishops in dioceses scattered across the globe are tasked with working *together* under the Pope's leadership to spread the Gospel message and build up the Kingdom of God announced by Jesus. This joint decision-making of the Pope and the bishops is called *Collegiality*.

In Ireland there are four Archdioceses (or Provinces): *Armagh* (North), *Dublin* (East), *Cashel* (South) and *Tuam* (West). In all they contain *twenty-six* separate dioceses (see map). Each diocese is subdivided into a number of *parishes*.

The Catechism and Canon Law

The members of the Catholic Church can refer to many written documents as sources of authority, most notably, the detailed *Catechism of the Catholic Church* published in 1994. This gives a comprehensive account of Catholic doctrine.

Map of Catholic
Diocesan boundaries.
➡

There are Vatican documents on all subjects. These range from how to
interpret the Bible, to how to approach new developments in human
reproduction.

There is a strict code of law, known as *canon law*, which relates to all church
matters and is interpreted by trained and appointed canon lawyers.

Guidance

The Catholic Church teaches that the Bible is *the inspired word of God*.
However, it points out that there are matters on which the Bible does not
always offer a clear answer. It needs to be *interpreted*.

The Catholic Church teaches that it is the true interpreter of the Bible. The Pope and the bishops have been entrusted with a mission to *clarify* and *interpret* the meaning of the scriptures. In this they are guided by the Holy Spirit.

When Catholics are seeking to understand the scriptures or trying to make a *moral decision* (i.e. considering what is the right thing to do), they are expected to carefully consider the teachings of the Church. These teachings represent two thousand years of accumulated wisdom.

[This is a topic to which we shall return in Book Three]

QUESTIONS

1. What does the Catholic Church teach about *all baptised people*?
2. (a) What is meant by the *Apostolic succession*?
   (b) How is it passed on?
3. (a) What is the role of the Pope in the Catholic Church?
   (b) Why is the Pope referred to as *the Vicar of Christ*?
4. What did the First Vatican Council teach about the Pope's authority?
5. How is the Pope elected?
6. What is a *cardinal*?
7. Explain the role of a *bishop* in a diocese.
8. What is *collegiality*?
9. Name the four archdioceses in Ireland.
10. What is *canon law*?
11. Name the book, published in 1994, in which people can find a comprehensive account of Catholic doctrine.
12. Explain the teaching of the Catholic Church with regard to interpreting the Bible.

Priests and Religious

Each parish is served by a *priest*, i.e. a man who has been *ordained* by a bishop. The priest is expected to:

■ administer the sacraments

■ give witness to the love of God by his presence and example

■ explain the Church's teaching by sermon or in discussion.

There are also *religious orders* within the Church. These consist of men and women, usually referred to respectively as *Brothers* and *Sisters*. They take solemn *vows* (i.e. promises) of poverty, chastity and obedience. They are expected to devote their lives to prayer, teaching and caring for the elderly, the sick and those on the margins of society.

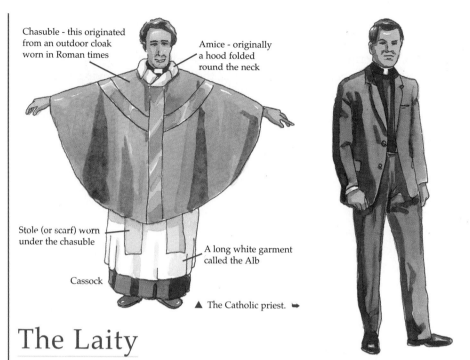

Chasuble - this originated from an outdoor cloak worn in Roman times

Amice - originally a hood folded round the neck

Stole (or scarf) worn under the chasuble

A long white garment called the Alb

Cassock

▲ The Catholic priest. ➡

The Laity

The vast majority of Catholics, are *lay people*, i.e. they are *not* ordained as priests. With the priest, they come together to celebrate their faith in the sacraments. Both lay people and clergy are called to give *witness* to God's love by what they say and do in the ordinary surroundings of everyday life. **See Chart**

The Body of Christ

The Church teaches that *all* its members are equal before God. The Pope, the bishops, priests, religious and lay people *together* form the Church – or as it has been described, the *Body of Christ* – on Earth. Encouraged and strengthened by the Holy Spirit, the Church is *one*, *holy*, *catholic* (worldwide) and *apostolic* (i.e. all its members are expected to make Jesus Christ known in daily life).

QUESTIONS

1. Explain the role of the *priest* in a parish.
2. What are the *religious orders* in the Catholic Church?
3. Explain the meaning of each of the following:
   (a) *the Body of Christ*
   (b) *catholic* and (c) *apostolic*.

LAY PEOPLE ARE CALLED TO

EXPLAIN THE PRINCIPLES WHICH CHRIST TAUGHT BY → READING IN CHURCH → MISSIONARY WORK → TEACHING

DEFEND CHRIST'S TEACHING THROUGH → HOPE PRAYER → FAITH → LOVE

APPLY CHRIST'S TEACHINGS TO THE PROBLEMS OF OUR TIME → VIOLENCE → DRUGS → CRIME

→ FEED THE HUNGRY → HOUSE THE HOMELESS → HEAL THE SICK

IN THE PARISH A LAY PERSON

SUPPORTS THE PRIEST BY → PRAYER → GIVING OUT COMMUNION → READING AT MASS

CO-OPERATES IN PRESENTING THE WORD OF GOD TO THE PARISH BY → INSTRUCTING → SUPPORTING e.g. SOCIETY OF ST VINCENT DE PAUL → COUNSELLING e.g. ACCORD

OFFERS SPECIAL SKILLS E.G. → BUILDING → YOUTH CLUBS → MANAGEMENT AND ACCOUNTING

SHARES PROBLEMS, E.G. → MARRIAGE PROBLEMS → DRINK → SICKNESS DEATH

↞ Following Christ in today's world.

JOURNAL WORK

Do you know of any parish-based voluntary group(s) which, by answering certain needs in the community, make(s) Jesus Christ known in daily life? Perhaps your class could invite a guest speaker to talk about his/her work.

CHAPTER ELEVEN

PROTESTANTISM AND ECUMENISM

Introduction

The principal Protestant Churches in Ireland are:

- The Church of Ireland
- The Presbyterian Church
- The Methodist Church
- The Baptist Church
- The Society of Friends
- The Salvation Army

We shall examine each briefly in turn.

The Church of Ireland

- The Church of Ireland is one of eighteen national churches in the *Anglican Communion*, i.e. the worldwide fellowship of independent churches derived from the Church of England.

- The Church of England was formed in the sixteenth century for a mixture of political and religious reasons. King Henry VIII wanted to have his marriage to Queen Catherine *annulled* (i.e. declared to have never happened) so that he could be free to marry

Henry VIII, founder of the Anglican Church.
➡

Anne Boleyn. When the Pope refused to allow this, Henry rejected the authority of the Pope and declared himself head of the Church in England, or as it is also known, the *Anglican Church*.

The spread of the British Empire took the teachings of the Church of England with it to Ireland, North America, Africa, India, Australia and New Zealand. Eventually, however, the Anglican churches in each country became independent, but they still retain links with the Church of England.

- It is difficult to summarise Anglican teaching because it is a *broad* movement with different groups within it. However, in 1920, it was agreed that the Apostle's Creed and the Nicene Creed express the fundamentals of the Christian faith.

- The *General Synod* is the chief decision-making body of the Church of Ireland. It meets every year for three days. It consists of two sections:
  (i) the House of Bishops (with twelve to fourteen members)
  and
  (ii) the House of Representatives (with two hundred and sixteen clergy and four hundred and thirty-two lay members)

- In recent times, the Church of Ireland has ordained women to the ministry. A Church of Ireland clergyman or clergywoman is usually referred to as a *rector* in his/her parish.

▲ Queen Elizabeth II and the Archbishop of Canterbury.

The Presbyterian Church

- This is a worldwide church especially strong in Scotland and Northern Ireland.

- It was started in the sixteenth century by John Calvin in Geneva. His ideas were brought to Scotland by John Knox in 1559 and to Ireland by planters in the seventeenth century.

- Both Calvin and Knox *rejected* the Pope's authority and the idea of bishops. They claimed that such

A clerical collar, sometimes with only the front part showing

An academic hood - showing that the minister has studied at a college

A plain black gown sometimes called a Geneva Gown, since the tradition came from there that ministers should wear them

Preaching bands - white strips of cloth hanging down from the collar, a sign that he is authorised to preach

A plain black scarf

Sometimes the costume is worn over a black cassock (as worn by Catholics also), but more often over ordinary clothes

◄ A Presbyterian minister.

things could not be found in the Bible. They wanted a church governed at local level by elders or *presbyters*, instead of bishops. Hence the name *Presbyterian* Church.

■ At national level, the *General Assembly* is the chief decision-making body. It appoints a *Moderator* as its chairperson and principal spokesman.

■ Presbyterian Churches are simple buildings. There are neither stained-glass windows nor any pictures or statues displayed.

■ A great love of the Bible is encouraged. Presbyterians consider themselves to be *people of the Book.*

The Methodist Church

▲ John Wesley.

■ This was founded in the eighteenth century by two Anglican clergymen – John Wesley and his brother Charles Wesley. They founded a movement aimed at reviving the Anglican Church, which they believed was losing touch with the needs of ordinary people.

■ John and Charles Wesley faced considerable opposition to their work from the leadership of the Church of England. Their followers were nicknamed *Methodists* because of their very *methodical* (i.e. *orderly*) approach to prayer, to the study of the Bible and to life in general.

■ By the end of the eighteenth century, these Methodists separated from the Church of England and formed a new *denomination* (i.e. separate branch) of the Christian tree.

■ As with the Presbyterian Church, the Methodist Church is *non-episcopal*, i.e. there are no bishops in authority. A council of Church members makes decisions and forms policy about Church organisation. A *moderator* is elected to act as chairperson and spokesperson.

■ Methodism teaches that all Christians are of equal status. No one is marked out as having a special ministry such as priesthood. Anyone, male or female, can be called by God to become a *minister.*

■ Often a minister has to look after a number of churches, so a system of trained church members exists to lead services and to preach to the congregation.

QUESTIONS

1. What is the *Anglican communion*?
2. Why did the Church of England split from the Catholic Church?
3. Explain the role and organisation of the *General Synod* of the Church of Ireland.
4. What is a *rector*?
5. Explain the origins of the name *Presbyterian*.
6. Who brought Presbyterianism to Scotland?
7. What is the role of the *moderator* of the Presbyterian Church?
8. Describe the interior of a Presbyterian Church.
9. Who founded the Methodist Church? Why?
10. Explain the origins of the name *Methodist*.
11. What is meant by saying that the Methodist Church is *non-episcopal*?

The Baptist Church

■ One of the issues debated during the Reformation of the sixteenth century was the subject of baptism. Some Christians in the Netherlands became convinced that the traditional practice of baptising babies was wrong. They believed that only adults should be baptised. They argued that only those who could make a conscious decision to follow Jesus should be baptised.

▲
A Baptist church in Tennessee, USA.

■ These particular Protestants became known as *anabaptists* (*ana* is the Greek word for *again*) because adults who had already been baptised as babies were being baptised again. This time they were being baptised by the method of *total immersion* (i.e. where the whole body goes under the water). They did this to represent the ending or death of their old life and a fresh, new beginning as a follower of Jesus Christ.

■ Gradually anabaptists became known simply as *Baptists*. They established themselves as a separate Protestant denomination. In 1611 they spread to England and from there to Ireland and North America.

■ Each Baptist congregation is self-governing. Baptists teach the *priesthood of all believers*. There are neither bishops nor priests. A council of lay members makes decisions affecting all aspects of church life.

The Society of Friends

■ In seventeenth century England, a small group of Christians led by George Fox became dissatisfied with all existing Church systems, whether Catholic or Protestant.

They believed that religion means each person following his/her personal conviction. They held that *all* formal church structures and ministers were *unnecessary*. They decided to call themselves the Society of Friends, though they are better known as the *Quakers*.

■ The name *Quaker* was a nickname given to Fox himself by Justice Bennett in 1650, after Fox had told the judge to *quake in fear at the word of the Lord*.

■ The Friends were persecuted by Anglicans and other Protestant denominations. An estimated fifteen thousand Quakers are thought to have died for their faith between 1650 and 1698. Despite this, the Friends were, and still remain, *pacifists*, i.e. they refuse to use violence or take part in any fighting force.

■ As a result of persecution, the Friends settled in North America in large numbers. One of their leading figures, William Penn, founded the colony of Pennsylvania as an experiment in *religious toleration* (i.e. people of different religions living side by side in peace).

■ The Friends have always had a great concern for social justice. They did much to help the sick and starving poor of Ireland when the Great Famine devastated the island in the late 1840s.

■ The Friends have neither ministers nor sacred buildings. They gather together in *meeting houses* to worship God *informally*. Their worship consists of long periods of silent prayer and reflection. They believe that the will of God for each person can be discovered in this way.

The Salvation Army

■ This was founded in 1865 by William Booth, a Methodist minister who worked in the terrible slums of Victorian London.

■ Booth dedicated his life to the poorest of the poor. Seeing the damage caused by alcohol abuse, he introduced a *total ban* on the consumption of *alcoholic drink* as part of the movement's teachings.

- The Salvation Army is organised on military lines. The minister is called an *officer*. The members are *soldiers*. All wear uniforms.
- Their meeting place for worship is called a *citadel*.
- The Salvation Army is highly regarded for its work among the poor and underprivileged.

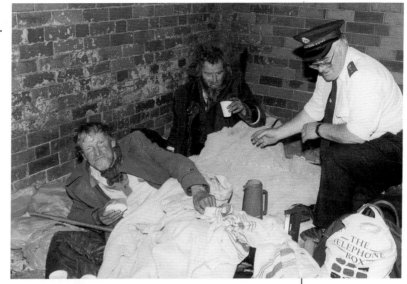

Salvation Army member caring for the homeless. ➡

QUESTIONS

1. Who are the Baptists?
2. Why were they originally known as *anabaptists*?
3. How did the Society of Friends come to be known as *the Quakers*?
4. What are *pacifists*?
5. Why did William Penn found the colony of Pennsylvania in America?
6. How did the Society of Friends reveal its great concern for social justice in Ireland in the 1840s?
7. Who founded the Salvation Army?
8. Why did he introduce a *ban* on alcohol consumption for its members?
9. In what way is the Salvation Army organised along military lines?

The Ecumenical Movement

The divisions within Christianity have tragically led to much conflict, bloodshed and persecution over the centuries. All of this has directly *contradicted* the teachings of Jesus Christ.

Since the early twentieth century, however, there has been a growing desire for better relations between the different Christian traditions. The attempt to foster a sense of *togetherness* across centuries-old divisions is referred to as the *ecumenical* movement (from the Greek work *oikumene* meaning *the whole world*).

The World Council of Churches

The ecumenical movement has its origins within the Protestant tradition. In 1910, an international conference was held in Edinburgh to discuss ways in which the different Protestant churches could work together in spreading the Christian faith in Africa and Asia. It was realised that divisions among Christians hindered the effort to spread the Gospel and to win new converts. Eventually, the World Council of Churches (WCC) was established in Geneva in 1945.

The WCC holds a general assembly every six years. It is attended by delegates from many countries. They discuss issues of common concern, such as:

- racism
- the plight of refugees
- the arms trade
- poverty
  and
- advances in technology.

The WCC has been marked by controversy. Some people have claimed that it has become too concerned with political issues. Others, however, say that it should be even more concerned with such matters.

At first, the Catholic Church and the Orthodox Churches were not represented at the WCC. However, the Orthodox Churches have been fully represented since 1961 and the Catholic Church has sent official observers since the general assembly of 1968.

The Catholic Church and Ecumenism

Since the Second Vatican Council (1962-1965), the Catholic Church has encouraged shared prayer and dialogue between its members and those of the other Christian traditions. There have been significant steps towards healing the rift between the Catholic Church and the Orthodox Churches.

Relations have also improved between the Catholic Church and those of many of the Protestant Churches. For example, the leaders of the different Christian churches in Northern Ireland have co-operated closely in recent years, praying together and producing joint statements.

Discussions have revealed much common ground between the Catholic Church and the Anglican Church. However, important differences remain on such issues as:

- the meaning of the sacraments
- the apostolic succession and
- the ordination of women.

▲
Leaders of different Christian traditions coming together in prayer for the first time in the 1960s.

The Future of the Ecumenical Movement

The whole thrust of the ecumenical movement is not to try to make all Christians the same. To do so would be to destroy what is distinctive in each tradition. Rather, its purpose is twofold:

- To promote mutual respect and understanding between the different Christian traditions

and

- To encourage Christians to co-operate with one another to fulfil the very purpose of the Christian community – to be *the Body of Christ* on earth – and to reveal the love of Christ to the whole world by what they say and do.

QUESTIONS

1. What is meant by *the ecumenical movement*?
2. Using the following words, fill in the spaces below.
   - assembly ■ Geneva ■ observers ■ six ■ 1961 ■ 1968

   The WCC was established in __ in 1945. It holds a general _____
   every ___ years. The Orthodox Churches have been represented since
   _____. The Catholic Church has sent official _____ since the general
   assembly of _____.
3. Identify *three* important areas where differences remain between the
   Catholic Church and the Anglican Church.

JOURNAL WORK

Invite a guest speaker from a particular Christian denomination to talk to
your class about his/her beliefs.

Part Four

Prayer and Worship

CHAPTER TWELVE

GROWING CLOSER TO GOD IN PRAYER

Introduction

Each of the major world religions:

- offers its own set of answers to questions about the meaning of life *and*
- seeks, in its own way, to guide people along the path of goodness.

However, only Judaism, Christianity and Islam teach that God – the source of all answers and guidance – is a *person* who *loves* us. As a result, these religions are deeply concerned with helping people to grow closer to God. This is done through *prayer*.

Meaning

Suppose you have a friendship with someone about whom you care a great deal. You always feel relaxed in his/her company. You can be yourself and feel confident that you are accepted and loved for who you are. You can *trust* this person.

However, consider what would happen if you stopped trying to make time to meet with your friend. What if you didn't spend time in each other's company? You know your friend cares for you, so you take that person for granted. You put him/her at the back of your mind. How long can your friendship survive this kind of treatment? Will it not eventually wither and fade away?

Yet, this is the kind of friendship many people, even many who say they are religious, have with *God*. They know deep down that God loves them, but they take it for granted. They never spend time with God. Even if they go to church their thoughts are somewhere *else*. They go about their daily lives with the view that God has no role to play in a dog-eat-dog world.

Genuinely religious people are those who believe that their relationship with God has *everything* to do with day-to-day living. It is their friendship with God that gives them the *strength* to face life's many challenges.

Building a true and lasting relationship with someone takes effort and long-term commitment. People need to devote time and energy to it. It is the same for their relationship with God. It needs *time, attention* and *care* if it is to grow and last.

Prayer is vitally important to building a strong and enduring friendship with God. Prayer has been described as

> *a conversation from the heart between God and human beings.*

Prayer has a twofold effect:
1) It strengthens people's awareness of God's loving presence in their lives.
2) It gives people a positive perspective on life and gives them the strength they need to face life's many challenges.

QUESTIONS

1. In what kind of God do Jews, Christians and Muslims believe?
2. A strong and lasting friendship requires those involved in it to commit themselves to do certain things to sustain it. What are these things?
3. Explain what is meant by *prayer* in your *own* words.
4. Read the following story:

   James Irwin, the American astronaut who piloted the Lunar Module on the Apollo 15 Moon mission, recounts his experience of prayer in his autobiography *To Rule the Night*.

   In this book, he talks about the overwhelming sense of the presence of God he had while he was on the Moon. He says that he felt that God was at his side, near to him as he worked. It was a feeling he had lost at home on Earth.

   He mentions one particular example while working on the Moon. He was working away from the module when a key cord broke, and he could not get his experimental station set up. He prayed and quickly found an answer. He said he felt as if God had pointed out the answer; helped him to figure out what to do. He did not check with his superiors at mission control as that would have delayed him. Anyway, he did not need their answer. He believed that *God* had already helped him. He knew what to do. He felt this very strongly.

   This experience convinced Irwin that God exists, a God on whom people can call at any time.

QUESTIONS CONT'D

Answer the following questions:
(a) When James Irwin talks about experiencing an *overwhelming sense of God's presence* when he was on the Moon, what does he mean?
(b) Irwin says that this experience convinced him of God's existence. In what kind of God does he believe?
(c) Describe your image of God.

Why Do People Pray?

Often people turn to God in prayer because they experience

■ suffering in their own lives;

■ sorrow for having let someone down in an important situation;

■ gratitude when something important goes well;

■ helplessness when they are powerless to help someone they love;

■ a sense of mystery and wonder through a loving relationship or an encounter with the beauty of nature;

■ how short and swiftly ended life can be.

Each of these different circumstances gives rise to a different kind of prayer. If we rearrange their order we can identify *six* types of prayer:
(1) *adoration* – a sense of mystery and wonder;
(2) *intercession* – love for other people and a wish to help them in practical ways;
(3) *petition* – an awareness of our own needs;
(4) *contrition* – a realisation of where we have gone wrong in our lives and a desire to live better lives;
(5) *protection* – a sense of the power of evil and an awareness of the suffering it causes;
(6) *thanksgiving* – a deep-seated gratitude to God for all those people and things that are important to us.

As we can see, prayer often consists of

■ giving thanks
■ giving praise
} *to* God

and

■ seeking help
■ seeking forgiveness } *from* God

A strong relationship with God gives a believer the strength to make the right choices in difficult situations and encourages him/her to follow the path of goodness.

Christians believe that, no matter what situations they may face, God is their companion and guide.

QUESTIONS

1. Select *any three* experiences from the six listed on page 99 which have led people to turn to God in prayer.
   In each case explain why you think that these experiences led them to do so.

2. Match the description in box *B* with the type of prayer in box *A*.

A	B
(i) Adoration	love for other people and a wish to help them
(ii) Intercession	a realisation of where we have gone wrong in our lives
(iii) Petition	a sense of the power of evil and a realisation of the suffering it causes
(iv) Contrition	a deep-seated gratitude for all those people and things that are important to us.
(v) Protection	a sense of mystery and wonder
(vi) Thanksgiving	an awareness of our own needs

3. A World War Two veteran once remarked that
   There are no atheists on a battlefield!
   What did he mean? What does this say about many people's attitudes to belief in God and to prayer?

How Do People Pray?

A person can pray to God on his/her own (read *Matthew* 6:5-6). A person should, however, pray with other members of his/her religious community on a regular basis. Worshipping together as a community helps to keep people's faith alive because it reminds them that their prayer life cannot be separated from other areas of their life.

A person cannot be a friend of God, if he/she ignores the needs of those around him/her.

Prayer itself can take many different forms. For instance:

■ **Vocal prayer**

People can recite a *formal* prayer, i.e. one with a fixed format that has been taken from the sacred scriptures (e.g. *Our Father* or *Hail Mary*) or one decided upon by religious authorities (e.g. *Apostles Creed*).

Or, people can say an *informal* prayer, i.e. one which they compose themselves.

People can also *sing* hymns or *play* an instrumental piece of music. The great Christian thinker, Augustine of Hippo, once wrote that:

> *To sing is to pray twice.*

■ **Silent prayer**

People can silently read and reflect or *meditate* on a passage of sacred scripture and see how its message can be applied to their daily lives.

When It Is Difficult To Pray

Even when people want to pray, they can often find it difficult to do so. If they are upset about something or if they have had a row with someone, they can find it difficult to concentrate. Their thoughts seem to crowd in. Since it is not possible to exclude them from their minds, the best thing is to *include* these thoughts in their prayers.

> *'Lord, I had a row with X today. I am very upset. My mind keeps going back to the quarrel and she was wrong. But was she? Isn't that my pride speaking? And even if she was wrong, am I not ready to forgive? Lord, how often have I wronged others, how often have I wronged you? You did not hold back your forgiveness so why should I now? Help me, Lord, to make the first step, to hold out a hand of friendship. She probably feels as bad about it as I do. Lord, give me the courage to forgive.'*
>
> T. McGivern, *Day-dreaming or Praying?*

A distraction need not be a distraction. It can help us to grow closer to God and to find the courage to show forgiveness and kindness. This is real prayer.

Meditation

Read the following extract:

> Most of us in our contemporary, fast-paced society are restless human beings. When faced with a chance to just be quiet for a while, we typically fidget or jump up to do something like turn on the television or play a computer game. We let our thoughts race through our heads like cars on a motorway. We prefer noise over silence, motion over stillness, being scattered over being focused. We desperately need to calm down and get ourselves together.

'Be still and know that I am God.' *Psalm* 46:10.

Meditation is an inner quieting so that a person can come together within and focus attention on something. You may have heard of meditation as a way for athletes to boost their performances, or for business executives to refresh their minds in the midst of a hectic workday. Doctors even recommend meditation to patients as a way to reduce stress and lower their blood pressure.

Those are all good uses of meditation. However, as a form of prayer, **Christian meditation** has a different purpose. Its goal is to focus on God and the mystery of God's love given to us in Jesus, using our thoughts, feelings, and imagination. That kind of focus requires inner quieting, much like the calming and centring techniques people might do to reduce stress and improve their work performance. But Christian meditation aims to clear 'inner space' for us *to make room for God in our heart*. It is not about achieving something like health or success but about consciously growing closer to God.

A passage in the Tenakh describes well what it means to meditate. 'Be still, and know that I am God!' (*Psalm* 46:10). If you have ever tried to empty your mind of thoughts, you know how difficult being still can be. It takes self-discipline, practice, and patience to learn how to meditate.

The *first step* is to calm the body by consciously relaxing the muscles and breathing deeply and rhythmically. The *next step* is to introduce some way of focusing attention. A method might be as simple as slowly repeating a word, like *Jesus* or *love*. Or one might read a Bible passage and reflect on it. Or put oneself into a

Gospel story as one of the characters, imagining one's feelings and reactions toward Jesus.

Sometimes meditation is so deep that it is purely an experience of the heart – no thoughts or words at all, just the sense of being in union with God. This type of meditation is called **contemplation.**

Adapted from : T. Zanzig and B. Allaire,
Understanding Catholic Christianity.

QUESTIONS

1. Identify some of the distractions with which people often fill their lives.
2. What is *meditation*? Why do doctors recommend it?
3. What is the purpose of *Christian* meditation?
4. In order to be able to meditate, a person must be willing to do certain things. What are they?
5. State the two steps in meditation identified in the extract.
6. What is *contemplation*?

The Lord's Prayer

The *Lord's Prayer*, or the *Our Father* is the only example in the *New Testament* of a prayer taught by Jesus himself. It has been described as the most perfect of prayers because it beautifully expresses so much of Jesus' teaching. We find two versions of it in the *New Testament*. A shorter one in *Luke* 11:2-4 and the more familiar longer version in *Matthew* 6:7-16.

THE LORD'S PRAYER

1. Our Father, who art in heaven,

2. hallowed be thy name.

3. Thy kingdom come. Thy will be done on earth, as it is in heaven.

4. Give us this day our daily bread,

5. and forgive us our trespasses, as we forgive those who trespass against us,

6. and lead us not into temptation, but deliver us from evil.

1. **Our Father who art in Heaven**
   Jesus surprised many of his followers by talking about God as a loving Father, and by referring to God as his Father in a most familiar way. He often used the terms *your heavenly Father* or *my Father*. In the parable of the prodigal son, the character of the boy's father was meant to describe God's attitude towards anyone who is a *sinner*; i.e. someone who has turned away from God.

   This story perfectly summarises the heart of Christian teaching about God. In other religions we see people seeking God. But in Christianity we see *God* reaching out to human beings first. The father did not wait for his son to reach him, rather *he went out* and greeted his son.

   However, God's love does not end at our death. God invites us to share eternal life with him.

2. **hallowed be thy name**
   'Hallow' is a word which means *'to honour as holy'*. Christians praise and honour God's holy name. They do this because praise is an important act of worship. They also honour God's name because it is an aspect of their religion which has come down from the Jewish religion. One of the Commandments is *Do not take the name of God in vain*. In ancient religions the name of God was a powerful word in worship. As a result of this Commandment, the Jews never spoke the name of God. Jesus took away the fear of the Commandment by praising the name of God. Christians generally disapprove of people who use the names *'God'*, or *'Jesus Christ'* etc. in a casual way, or as a way of expressing surprise or anger. They consider such behaviour as being disrespectful.

3. **Thy Kingdom come, thy will be done, on earth as it is in heaven**.
   Christians believe that God takes care of all that he has created. They use the title of *King* to describe his status over all humankind. The *Kingdom of Heaven* was described by Jesus in parables like the mustard seed, the hidden treasure, or the fine pearl. He told his disciples that the parables gave them *the secret of the Kingdom of God* (*Mark* 4:11). The *Old Testament* spoke about the Messiah bringing the Kingdom of God, and Jesus demonstrated in his life what it would mean for God to reign in the hearts of all people. That is why Christians work very hard to remove the injustice, poverty and violence which prevent the world from being what God intended when he created it. Christians

are convinced that this can only happen when people live according to the teaching and example of Jesus who came to show people what God is like. Christians are helped by their belief in the goodness of God, to accept suffering and to say *thy will be done*.

4. **Give us this day our daily bread**

Jesus uses *bread*, which is a basic food that supports human life, to explain his teaching about God. He multiplied bread for the crowds who followed him. He said, *'I am the bread of life'*; *'the one who eats this bread will live for ever'* (John 6:35, 51). In the Lord's Prayer 'daily bread' represents all the needs of God's people, and is an example of the prayer of petition, or request, which is one of the main types of Christian prayer. This request also recognises that we should give *thanks* to God from whom all good things (e.g. food) ultimately come.

5. **and forgive us our trespasses as we forgive those who trespass against us**

A trespass is an offence against a person, a law, a principle or a right. Christians speak about *sins* (i.e. wrongdoing), and they believe that Jesus was the *Lamb of God* whose life and death made up for the *sin* of the whole world. Asking for forgiveness (i.e. sorrow for sin) is another important feature of the Christian prayer. The parable of the unforgiving servant was told by Jesus in answer to Peter's question: *'Lord, if my brother keeps on sinning against me, how many times do I have to forgive him?'* (Matthew 18:21)

Forgiveness of others is an important condition for personal forgiveness in Christian prayer and everyday life situations.

6. **and lead us not into temptation, but deliver us from evil**

Christians believe in the power of God over evil. They believe that they can draw on God's love to strengthen them in times of crisis and temptation. They believe that the power of sin and death were overcome by the life, death and resurrection of Jesus.

Section entitled *The Lord's Prayer* includes information adapted from:
Sr Helen Burke, *Dimensions of Christianity*.

QUESTIONS

1. Match each explanation in Box *B* with the appropriate statement from the *Lord's Prayer* in Box *A*.

A	B
Our Father, who art in heaven,	People should work with God for the coming of the Kingdom.
hallowed be thy name.	God will provide us with what we need.
Thy kingdom come, thy will be done on earth as it is in heaven.	God is the Father (i.e. loving parent) of all people and he invites all people to share eternal life with him.
Give us this day our daily bread	God is to be trusted. God will strengthen people in times of crisis and temptation.
and forgive us our trespasses as we forgive those who trespass against us	God's name is to be respected.
and lead us not into temptation, but deliver us from evil.	Being forgiven by God depends upon forgiving those who have offended us.

2. The *Lord's Prayer* is a beautiful summary of all Christian prayer. It contains prayers of:
   - praise
   - sorrow
   - thanksgiving
   - petition.

   Read it once more and find an example of each of these four kinds of prayer.

Does God Listen?

Sometimes people think that their prayers are not answered, that God does not listen to them. But is this the case? Consider the following:

1 *Doing our part*

Some people have a *magical* view of prayer. They do not realise that to pray for something means that they must be prepared to play *their* part in bringing it about.

For example, if a person became seriously ill, he/she might pray for the strength to endure the pain and worry of it. But he/she would still go to a *doctor*, follow the advice given and undergo medical treatment. He/she would have to *co-operate* with those trying to treat the illness.

Christians believe that to pray for something, be it a cure from illness or passing an exam, means that a person is committing him/herself to living up to his/her own responsibilities.

As Bishop Donal Murray has written:

When Christians pray 'Thy Kingdom come', they are making a commitment. They are recognising an obligation to work for the Kingdom of God and to create among people the sort of relationships which are acceptable to God.

2 *Being willing to change*

Sometimes prayers may go unanswered because people's own behaviour may be getting in the way of God's answer. They are not willing to play their part, when to get what they want would involve a change in their way of life. They do not want to make the effort needed.

God has given human beings the gift of *free will*. Having given this gift, God will *not* take it away. Rather, God asks people to use this gift wisely – to choose good rather than evil. Jesus taught that God wants people to work together with him to build a better world.

God does listen to human beings. But so too should people listen to what God is saying.

QUESTIONS

1 Explain what it means to say that
   Some people have a magical view of prayer.
2 What is the importance for prayer of people being willing to:
   (a) play their part in making something happen,
       and
   (b) change the way they live their lives?

QUESTIONS CONTD

3 Read the story of the Rich Young Man in *Mark* 10:17-23.
What is the point of this story?
What does it say about the way people should approach prayer?

On Being Hopeful

Sometimes, however, it can be very difficult to see any reason for hope, particularly when we see how bad things can happen to those who least deserve them.

Consider the story of the great American president, Abraham Lincoln. In his life he endured much disappointment and suffering.

Mark Link SJ writes:

Abraham Lincoln knew failure. For thirty years it dogged his every footstep. It walked the streets with him during the day. It kept him awake at night.
A partial list of his failures reads like this:

1832	defeated in the election for the legislature
1833	failed in business
1836	nervous breakdown
1843	defeated in nomination for Congress
1854	defeated for Senate
1856	defeated in nomination for vice-president

▲
The Abraham Lincoln Memorial, Washington D.C.

However, in 1860, Abraham Lincoln was elected President of the United States.

Abraham Lincoln was well prepared for the defeats and setbacks that battered and bruised America during the terrible Civil War years. A lesser man would have collapsed under the enormous strain of leading the country. Throughout it all, his faith in God gave him the strength to face each new challenge.

Of himself, Lincoln said: *'God selects his own instruments, and sometimes they are strange ones; for instance, he chose me to steer the ship through a great crisis.'*

Prayer is not so much a matter of persuading God to do things, rather it is more a matter of people agreeing to put their *trust* in God's plan for the world. However, people's faith in God is often challenged by their experience of suffering and evil. They ask: '*Why would a loving God put human beings in a world where they have to suffer?*'

This is an important question which raises complex issues we will examine in *Book Three*. Traditionally, Christians have responded to it by saying that '*God's ways are not our ways*'. Ultimately, only God knows the full reasons for the existence of suffering and evil. Christians remember how Jesus, as he knelt in prayer in the Garden of Gethsemane, was frightened by the pain he knew he would have to endure.

Yet, he said: *Not my will but yours be done.*

Luke 22:42.

This is the great challenge of prayer. It demands *real, deep* trust in God's goodness.

QUESTIONS

1 What, do you think, people today can learn from Abraham Lincoln's life story? Explain your answer.

JOURNAL WORK

Having considered how and why people pray, compose your own prayer, which would be suitable for your present situation.

CHAPTER THIRTEEN

THE LANGUAGE OF WORSHIP: SIGN AND SYMBOL

Worship

All religions involve the worship of a God or gods. The word *worship* comes from the Old English word *weorthscipe,* which means *recognising worth.* The origin of the word itself provides a key to understanding the important role of worship in the life of the believer.

◄ *The Transfiguration*
by William Blake.

Worship has *three* elements:

■ It is a *recognition* of the supreme importance of God who is the creator and sustainer of the universe.

■ It is a *response* to the mysterious presence of God in people's lives through the offering of prayers of thanksgiving and praise.

■ It engages people in a *relationship* with God, as it is in God alone that people can find the answers to life's great mysteries.

Jews, Christians and Muslims believe that only God is worthy of worship and that to offer worship to anyone or anything other than God is *wrong*, and they refer to it as *idolatry*.

Idolatry is:

■ a breach of the First Commandment

■ a grave insult to God who *alone* is worthy of worship.

Ritual

A ritual may be defined as

> *a formal religious ceremony, approved by religious authorities, which gives a regular pattern to people's worship of God.*

Rituals celebrate the presence of God in people's lives. God, though real, is *invisible*. Rituals are concerned with making this non-physical reality *visible* and *accessible* to people.

In doing so, rituals perform *three* important functions:

■ They forge links between the worshipper and God.

■ They focus the worshipper's attention on God.

■ They depict or recall key events in the story of a religion.

These important functions are achieved through the use of sign and symbol.

QUESTIONS

1. Explain the origin of the word *worship*.
2. What is *idolatry*? Give an example of idolatry taken from everyday life.
3. Why do Jews, Christians and Muslims believe that idolatry is wrong?
4. What is a *ritual*?
5. State the *three* functions of a ritual.

Sign and Symbol

The words *sign* and *symbol* are often confused with one another. Sometimes they are used interchangeably, as if they mean exactly the same thing. They do *not*.

   The difficulty people experience in distinguishing between a sign and a symbol arises from the fact that each of them is

> *a concrete image or word or gesture intended to represent something beyond itself.*

On closer inspection, however, we can see how they differ from each other. We shall now clarify the meaning of each in turn.

Sign

A sign is a concrete image or word or gesture that points beyond itself *to only one fixed and definite meaning*.
   For example:

- A green light at a road junction is a simple sign that means 'proceed ahead'.
- A sign in a shop window that reads *SALE* gives a straightforward and unambiguous message.

In each of the above examples, the sign has only *one* meaning.
   Signs are useful abbreviations. Without them we would not be able to give clear, quick messages to each other.

Symbol

A symbol is *also* a concrete image or word or gesture that points beyond itself.

   However, a symbol has a *much richer content* than a sign. A symbol enables us to express ideas that are very difficult to put into words.

   For example, consider the experience of *joy*.

   Joy itself cannot be seen as it is *abstract*, i.e. it has no size, weight, colour or shape. It cannot be described like a concrete object such as a chair. But joy can be expressed in poetry, music or art through the use of *symbol*.

   A symbol is distinguished from a sign by the following three characteristics:

1 A symbol has *more* than one meaning.
Consider the lights on a Christmas tree, or a Christmas candle.

They are *symbols* because they remind people that

- Jesus, whose birth Christians celebrate at this time, is the *Light of the World*.
- Christmas is a time when those who have much should share generously with those who have little.
- Christmas is a holiday season intended to brighten the dark days of winter.

Symbols by their nature can never be confined or reduced to narrow one-dimensional meanings.

← A rocky mountain — symbol of steadfastness.

2 The meaning of a symbol is *discovered*, not imposed on it.
Consider a visible, tangible object such as a rock. It can be a *symbol* because it can help us to define our ideas about strength, enduring loyalty and steadfastness.

In this case a rock can be a symbol because we *discover* a vital *connection* between it and the things for which it stands.

▼ A gentle breeze stirring the grass — symbol of refreshment.

▼ Water — symbol of life.

**3 A symbol is not only thought-provoking but also strikes a deep
emotional chord within people.**

Consider how although road signs are important, it really doesn't matter
which signs are used, so long as motorists understand them.

A symbol, however, is different. It evokes a deeper response in us. A
symbol touches *both* the mind and the heart.

For example, a nation's flag usually includes certain colours and details
that symbolise or represent important beliefs about that country.

Consider the flag of the Republic of Ireland. It is a *tricolour*.

This design and these three colours were chosen to express an important
aspiration. Let us consider each colour in turn.

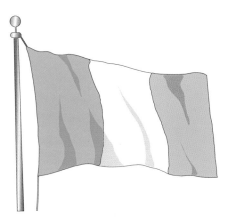

Green: represents the
Nationalist tradition

Orange: represents the Unionist
tradition

White: expresses unity.

The founders of our state hoped
that Ireland would be a place where
the members of both traditions,
Nationalist and Unionist, could live in
peace and mutual respect.

Our *awareness* of symbol is important, because it:

- enriches our experience of life by helping us to look more deeply and
  see beyond the surface of things
- enables us to discover the different meanings in things
- opens us up to the presence of God in our lives.

QUESTIONS

1. Why do people often have difficulty in distinguishing between a *sign*
   and a *symbol*?
2. What is a *sign*?
3. Draw and explain the meaning conveyed by any *four* signs that you
   pass on your way to and from school.
4. What is the *value* of signs?
5. Explain the meaning of the term *abstract*. Name *three* things other
   than *joy* that are abstract.

QUESTIONS CONTD

6. Briefly state the *three* characteristics that distinguish a symbol from a sign.
7. Describe or draw one symbol in which you feel *personally* involved. This could be a song, team badge, sculpture, or painting. Then explain the meaning that it has for you.
8. Why is our awareness of symbol important?

Christian Symbols

Christianity is rich in symbols. In *Book One* we noted how each evangelist has his own symbol:

- *Matthew* – an angel
- *Mark* – a lion
- *Luke* – an ox
- *John* – an eagle

Three common Christian visual symbols are:

- The Chi-Rho
  This is based on the first two letters of the Greek word for Christ – *Christos*.

Chi-Rho

- The IHS
  This is a monogram for the name of Jesus in Greek.

- INRI
  This is taken from the initial letters of *Iesus Nazarenus Rex Iudaeorum*, meaning *Jesus of Nazareth, King of the Jews*. This was the statement Pontius Pilate ordered to be placed on the cross. It reminds Christians of the suffering, death and resurrection of Jesus.

IHS

INRI

Perhaps the most popular symbol among early Christians was the *fish*. This was clearly an appropriate symbol:

- Some of the first disciples were fishermen. The apostle Peter, the first pope, was a fisherman.

■ Fish make many appearances in the Gospels:
- Parable of the Net (*Matthew* 13:47-50).
- Feeding of the Five Thousand (*Matthew* 14:13-21).
- Calling of the Disciples (*Luke* 5:1-11).
- Miraculous Catch of Fish (*John* 21:1-4).

But the early widespread use of the fish as a symbol runs deeper than this. The Greek word for fish is **Ichthys**. Each letter of the word points to a name or title of Jesus.

I	Iesos	Jesus	
Ch	Christos	Christ	Meaning:
Th	Theou	Of God	*Jesus Christ, God's Son,*
Y	Yios	Son	*Saviour.*
S	Soter	Saviour	

Early Christian paintings, particularly those in the catacombs beneath Rome, focus on the symbol of the fish and upon the idea of Jesus as the *Gentle Shepherd* of his people. The early Christians were reluctant to show Jesus on the cross because that was still a shameful death reserved for criminals. Later, of course, the cross became *the* Christian symbol above all others.

Without doubt, crucifixion was a cruel and vicious form of execution. So why did Christians choose to remember Jesus with such a symbol?

Jesus the Gentle Shepherd, Catacombs, Rome.

One reason is that the cross gives people a powerful *insight* into what God is like. God *understands* what it is to suffer. But more than this, on the cross God says

Not only do I know about your suffering, I have shared in it.

For people who are themselves suffering from illness or injustice, their belief in a loving God who suffers too can be a *lifeline*. It helps them to find *purpose* in their suffering, the *strength* to endure it, and the *hope* of eternal peace and joy with God beyond it.

The Cross

The cross is almost always found in a Christian place of worship. Here are three different forms of the cross:

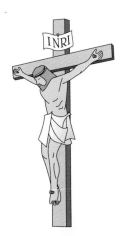

■ A *crucifix* is a cross with a figure or image of Jesus hanging from it, either dead or in agony. This represents the *suffering* of Jesus by which Christians believe they have been saved from sin and death.

■ A *plain* cross, i.e. one without a figure or image of Jesus upon it, emphasises the *resurrection* of Jesus which all Christians believe to be a promise of eternal life for them.

■ A *crucifix* which shows Jesus on the cross but *alive* and *in triumph*. He is dressed in the rich clothes of a king and wearing a crown. This expresses *both* the suffering and the resurrection of Jesus.

QUESTIONS

1. Draw the following visual symbols and explain their meaning:
   ■ the Chi-Rho
   ■ the IHS
2. What does *INRI* mean?
3. State *three* reasons why the *fish* is an appropriate symbol for Christianity.
4. Why were the early Christians reluctant to show Jesus on the cross?
5. Why did Christians choose to remember Jesus with the symbol of the *cross*?
6. What is a *crucifix*?
7. Explain the meaning of a *plain* cross.

JOURNAL WORK

As a group, put together a collage of pictures and words, taken from newspapers and magazines, which *symbolises* your particular class. Then, write a brief report on what you have learned.

CHAPTER FOURTEEN

GROWING CLOSER TO GOD IN THE SACRAMENTS

The Sense of the Sacred

At the heart of religion is the awareness that *beyond* the visible, tangible world in which we live, there is a God who gives meaning and purpose to our lives.

Mother Theresa of Calcutta.

For Christians, God is *not* remote. Indeed, as the poet Patrick Kavanagh once wrote, God is present in and communicates with us through *the bits and pieces of everyday*.

If we reflect upon all the people, places and events that affect our lives, we can see how each points *beyond* itself. Each act of human kindness and each experience of natural beauty can be understood as a *symbol*. Each in its own way *reveals* something of the goodness and greatness of God.

This awareness of the invisible presence of God in our lives is called *the sense of the sacred* (from the Latin word *sacer* meaning *holy*). It is expressed in *symbol* and celebrated in *ritual*.

The Importance of Ritual

Imagine declaring your love by offering a bouquet of flowers. If one flower from that bouquet was pressed between the pages of a book, it could represent, fifty years later, the whole history and depth of that love. But if some stranger opened the book and saw the flower, to him/her it would be meaningless – nothing but faded petals.

Whether it is love or religion, emotions fade from their first intensity, but scents and sounds and objects can, like the sight of a pressed flower, recall the intensity and depth of that first experience long ago. So too religions use *symbols*, i.e. words and gestures and images, in worship, to lead their members' minds back to their central beliefs and to act as a springboard for their prayer. For example, Catholics use symbols such as *bread, wine, oil* and *incense* in worship.

Over a period of time, a web of agreed symbols gradually builds up to become a body of *rituals*. These rituals are based on what first happened spontaneously, then was repeated frequently enough to be preserved for ever. Later, we shall consider the central ritual of the Catholic faith – *the Mass*.

Rituals are of great importance:

■ They are the collective memory of the community of believers.

■ They transmit the meaning of the religion to new generations.

■ They strengthen the identity of the community that gathers to worship.

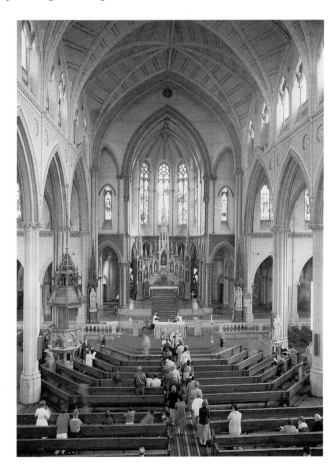

The Liturgy

The official public rituals of the Catholic Church are called the *liturgy*. The word *liturgy* comes from the Greek word *leitourgia* meaning *public service*, by which is meant the worship of God by the community.

The liturgy consists chiefly of the *seven sacraments*. As official public acts of the Catholic Church, these rituals have certain *fixed* features, although they can be modified in a limited way in special circumstances.

QUESTIONS

1. Explain what is meant by the statement: *Each act of human kindness and each experience of natural beauty can be understood as a symbol.*

2. Use the words listed below to fill in the missing words in the spaces provided.

   ■ meaning   ■ presence   ■ purpose   ■ ritual
   ■ sacred   ■ symbol   ■ tangible   ■ visible

   At the heart of religion is the awareness that beyond the _____ , _____ world in which we live, there is a God who gives _____ and _____ to our lives.

   This awareness of the invisible _____ of God in our lives is called the sense of the _____ . It is expressed in _____ and celebrated in _____ .

3. Explain the origin of the word *sacred*.

4. Why do religions use *symbols* (i.e. words, gestures and images) in worship?

5. Gestures are symbols people perform. Christians pray using certain gestures.

   Match the explanation in column *B* with the gesture in column *A*.
   Note the words in italics in column *A*. They provide a *clue*.

A GESTURE	B EXPLANATION
To pray with arms *outstretched* or hands held together.	To humbly acknowledge the greatness of God.
To pray standing *up*.	To remember the suffering and death of Jesus on the cross.
To kneel *down*.	To recall the resurrection of Jesus from the dead.

6. Why can such gestures be considered an *international* language of worship for Christians across the globe?

7. What is the importance of rituals?

8. What is the *liturgy*?
   Of what does the liturgy chiefly consist?

The Sacraments

As we saw in *Book One*, after his resurrection Jesus revealed that he was no longer limited by the physical laws of the universe that restrict our human freedom of action. For example:

- Jesus could appear suddenly in a locked room (see *John* 20:19).
- Jesus could vanish at will (see *Luke* 24:31).

The Incredulity of St Thomas by Morando.

Jesus revealed that he was free to be *present* at any time, in any place and as he chose to be present. This is a profound *mystery*.

The Gospels portray Jesus as continually seeking to share his love with people. Before his ascension, he promised his disciples that

> *I will be with you always.*
> *Matthew* 28:20.

Catholics believe that Jesus keeps this promise and that he is *present* today when they come together in his name to celebrate the *sacraments*. As he told the disciples:

> *Where two or three are gathered in my name, there am I in the midst of them.*
> *Matthew* 18:20.

The word *sacrament* comes from two Latin words: *sacramentum*, meaning solemn obligation, and *sacare*, meaning to set apart as holy or sacred.

There are seven sacraments:

■ Baptism

■ Confirmation

■ Eucharist

■ Reconciliation

■ Matrimony

■ Holy Orders

■ Anointing of the Sick

Emphasis on the seven sacraments is a distinctive feature of *both* the Catholic tradition *and* the Orthodox tradition. Most Protestants will acknowledge two sacraments only: Baptism and Eucharist. However, their understanding of these sacraments differs from that of the Catholic and Orthodox traditions.

The process whereby the Catholic Church recognised these seven sacraments took place over many centuries. The first Church council to officially name the seven sacraments was the Fourth Latern Council in 1215. However, it was not until the Council of Trent in 1547, that it was defined as being *a matter of faith* that there were *seven* sacraments.

These seven sacraments are *public rituals* in which Catholics recall and re-enact the life, death and resurrection of Jesus Christ. Indeed, Catholics believe that Jesus himself was the *first* sacrament. In his life, death and resurrection, Jesus *revealed* the glory of God's unlimited goodness in all he said and did. As the early Christians came to realise, Jesus was and *is Emmanuel*, i.e. *God-with-us*.

Christians believe that Jesus is present in the sacraments today. They believe that he comes to them in the visible symbols of bread, wine, oil and water. As Ambrose of Milan has written:

> *You have shown yourself to me Christ, face to face. I meet you in the Sacraments.*

The *Gospels* show how Jesus was always there to support and strengthen people at important times in their lives. In each of the sacraments, Catholics celebrate the presence of Jesus in the key moments of their lives today.

Baptism	birth
Confirmation	growth to maturity
Eucharist	living and sharing with others
Reconciliation	failure and forgiveness
Matrimony	marriage
Holy Orders	sacred ministry
Anointing	illness, healing and death

When Catholics participate in celebration of the sacraments, they are also giving an undertaking to make the presence of Jesus felt in their daily lives by the *example* they give to each other. The sacraments are *transformative events*, i.e. they are intended to bring about a change in people. However, they can only do so if people open their hearts and minds to God.

If people *offer* genuine, heartfelt *worship* to God in the sacraments, then they will *receive* God's *grace*, i.e. they will experience the loving presence of God in their lives. This nourishes and strengthens their faith.

The Catholic Church teaches that, through the presence of Jesus in the sacraments, people are:

- strengthened by the power of the Holy Spirit to live out their commitment to follow the example of Jesus in daily life.

- brought into fellowship with one another and joined together as a community of faith.

- encouraged to live in hope of a future life with God in heaven.

QUESTIONS

1. List the seven sacraments of the Catholic tradition.
2. What do members of the Protestant tradition believe about the sacraments?
3. What does it mean to say that *Jesus was the first sacrament*?
4. In what way do Catholics believe that Jesus is *present* to them in the sacraments today?
5. Match the key moments in people's lives in column *B* with the sacraments listed in column *A*.

A SACRAMENTS	B KEY
Baptism	failure and forgiveness
Confirmation	sacred ministry
Eucharist	illness, healing and death
Reconciliation	growth and maturity
Matrimony	birth
Orders	living and sharing with others
Anointing	marriage

6. When Catholics participate in the sacraments, what undertaking are they giving?
7. The *sacraments* are described as *transformative events*. What does this mean?

QUESTIONS CONTD

8. Use the words below to fill in the blank spaces provided.
   ■ genuine   ■ grace   ■ presence   ■ worship
   Catholics believe that if people offer _____ , heartfelt _____ to
   God in the sacraments, they will receive God's _____ , i.e. they
   will experience the loving _____ of God in their lives.

THE CROSS
This is the universal symbol
of Christianity.

STAINED GLASS
Some churches are richly decorated
with paintings, statues and stained
glass. For some Christians, beautiful
things inspire prayer and celebrate the
beauty of God.

THE TABERNACLE
This is a small safe which holds the Blessed
Sacrament. Catholics believe that the Blessed
Sacrament, i.e. the consecrated bread, not
consumed during Mass but reserved in the
tabernacle, is Jesus - really present, to be
honoured and adored. The Blessed Sacrament
is also called the Eucharist.

THE STATIONS OF THE CROSS

**SANCTUARY
LAMP**
This is lit to show
that Jesus is present.

**THE PULPIT OR
LECTERN**
This is where the
scriptures are read and
the sermon given.

THE ALTAR
This recalls the table
around which Jesus
and his disciples
gathered at the Last
Supper.

JOURNAL WORK

Read the following statement by Hugh Lavery, a Catholic writer, about the loss of religious faith in our society.

> *The disease of the Western world is an eye-disease, one which has narrowed vision so that people only see things as surface.*

(a) What point is he making here? In making your reply consider how *image-conscious* many people are today. Are people too taken-up with surface appearances only?

(b) What are the consequences of many people *seeing things as surface* for an appreciation of religious rituals such as the sacraments?

The Christian Year

For a Christian, the word *year* can have several different meanings. It can refer to

- the *calendar* year
- the *academic* year
- the *liturgical* year

The liturgical year is the *annual journey*, through religious rituals, in which Christians recall the events in the life of Jesus Christ and the beginnings of the Christian religion. However, the liturgical year is more than a *commemoration* of past events. It is also a *celebration* of Jesus Christ living in the Church today and an *invitation* to grow closer to him in worship.

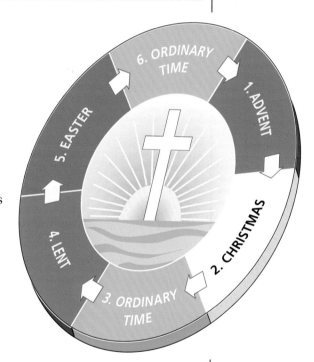

Advent

The Christian year begins with the season of *Advent*, from the Latin *adventus* meaning *the coming*. For four weeks before Christmas, Christians reflect on the coming of Jesus Christ:

- in the *past*   two thousand years ago in Bethlehem
- in the *present*   through the sacraments and the people they encounter
- in the *future*   when he will return at the end of time to bring to completion the Kingdom of God on Earth.

➤ The light of the
Advent wreath
reminds us that
Christ is coming.

During Advent, Christians examine their lives and prepare to celebrate Jesus' birth. They seek to demonstrate their love for him through generosity and forgiveness of one another.

Christmas

Christmas is the season in which the birth of Jesus is celebrated. The *feast* of Christmas itself is set on 25 December and this is a holy day of obligation for Catholics (i.e. they are required to attend mass).

The word Christmas comes from the Old English expression *Cristes Maesse*, meaning *the Mass of Christ*. For Catholics it begins with a vigil or evening mass on 24 December.

The Christmas season includes the feast of *Epiphany*, from the Greek, meaning *to show forth*. It is celebrated on 6 January. It recalls the worship of Jesus by the wise men, three non-Jews who recognised Jesus as the saviour of *all* humankind (see *Matthew* 2:1-12). This feast also reminds Christians to think of life as a great journey. Just as the wise men trusted the star to lead them, so too should people allow Jesus to guide them through life.

The Christmas season ends on the Sunday following the Epiphany when Catholics recall and celebrate the baptism of Jesus and the beginning of his public ministry.

Ordinary Time

Ordinary Time covers about sixty per cent of the liturgical year. It is divided into *two* periods as shown in the diagram on page 127. The *first* is between Christmas time and Lent. The *second* is between Easter and the next Advent.

Each week during Ordinary Time, the liturgy focuses on a different aspect of Jesus' life and teachings. The Gospel readings portray Jesus teaching in parables and performing miracles.

Lent

The season of *Lent* lasts for forty days. It recalls the time Jesus spent in the wilderness before beginning his public ministry. Lent is a time of preparation for Easter. This preparation usually includes

- prayer and reflection
- fasting and self-discipline
  and
- good works (i.e. helping others).

Lent is not only about giving up things, but about doing something *positive* and *creative*.

Lent begins on *Ash Wednesday* when Catholics attend mass and are marked on their foreheads with ashes. This is done to remind them that, though following Jesus involves suffering, the way of the cross is the way to new life, to resurrection with Jesus.

The last week of Lent is called *Holy Week*. The days of this week have a special importance in the Christian calendar: *Palm Sunday*, *Holy Thursday*, *Good Friday* and *Holy Saturday*.

Blessing with ashes on Ash Wednesday.

Easter

Although many people today highlight the celebration of Christmas, the *Easter* season is *the heart* of the liturgical year. This is because all the other

The Lighting of the Paschal Candle at the Easter Vigil.

events in Jesus' life, from his birth to his ascension are important *because* he died and rose from the dead. The celebration of Easter sheds its light on the whole Christian year. Through his death and resurrection Jesus showed that sin and death can be overcome and that all people can have the opportunity to be happy with God forever.

In the Catholic and Orthodox traditions, the celebration of Easter begins with the Mass of the Vigil, which takes place in the hours of darkness on Holy Saturday evening. *Easter Sunday* is a *moveable feast* in the Catholic Church. This means that it is celebrated on a Sunday between 22 March and 25 April.

Forty days after Easter Sunday is the feast of *the Ascension,* which marks the day when Jesus ceased to appear to his disciples and returned to his heavenly Father. Then, ten days later, Christians celebrate the feast of *Pentecost*, which is sometimes called the *birthday of the Christian religion.* Christians recall how the Holy Spirit descended upon his disciples and gave them the courage they needed to publicly preach Jesus' message. Christians pray that the power of God will transform their lives too, so that they will grow ever closer to God.

QUESTIONS

1. What is the *Liturgical year*?
2. Why is the liturgical year described as
   ■ a *commemoration*,   ■ a *celebration*   and   ■ an *invitation*?
3. What is the name given to the four weeks of preparation for Christmas?
4. On what day of the year do Christians celebrate the Incarnation?
5. What is meant by a *holy day of obligation*?
6. Explain the meaning of the following words:
   (a) *Christmas* and (b) *Epiphany*.
7. (a) What is *Ordinary Time*?
   (b) When does it occur in the liturgical year?
   (c) On what do the Gospel readings focus in Ordinary Time?
8. How long is the season of Lent?
9. What preparations for Easter are Catholics expected to make during Lent?
10. Why do Catholics have their foreheads marked with ashes on Ash Wednesday?
11. What is the name given to the last week of Lent?

QUESTIONS CONTD

12. (a) Name the most important Christian festival.
    (b) Why is it considered to be *the heart* of the liturgical year?
13. Name the festival which marks the return of Jesus to God his Father.
14. The word *Pentecost* means *fifty*. Why do you think this is the name given to the feast that recalls the descent of the Holy Spirit on the disciples?

CHAPTER FIFTEEN

SACRAMENTS OF INITIATION I: BAPTISM AND CONFIRMATION

Baptism

Introduction

There is a tradition among Catholics of dipping the right hand into a water-font and making the sign of the cross when entering and leaving a church. This gesture is intended to remind Catholics of the first sacrament they receive – *baptism*.

Baptism is the first of three *sacraments of initiation*, namely *Baptism, Confirmation* and *Eucharist*. They are called *sacraments of initiation*, because each of them represents a *stage* in the process towards *full membership* in both the Catholic tradition and the Orthodox tradition.

Meaning

The sacrament of baptism has its origin in the baptism of Jesus. The word itself comes from the Greek word *baptizo* meaning *to dip*.

The sacrament of baptism may be received only *once*. It may be administered in either of *two* ways:

■ by *infusion* – where a little water is poured over the person's head

■ by *immersion* – where the entire person is dipped into water.

QUESTIONS

1. Name the *three* sacraments of initiation.
2. Why are they called *sacraments of initiation*?
3. What is the origin of the word *baptism*?
4. State the two ways in which the sacrament of baptism may be administered.

History

Until the middle of the fifth century A.D., most *catechumens* (i.e. candidates for baptism) were adults. They had to undergo a long period of preparation. This is still required of adults who *convert* from non-Christian religions today.

➤ The exterior of the baptistry in Florence, Italy. This was built in 1400. At that time entire buildings were set aside for baptisms.

Some Christian denominations, such as the Baptists, will only baptise adults. In the Catholic and Orthodox traditions, however, infants are baptised. This change was introduced from the fifth century onwards. This was done so that:

■ the family could celebrate the arrival of the baby, hold a formal naming ceremony and give thanks to God for the gift of this precious new life.

■ the Church as a community could welcome the arrival of a new member into its family of faith.

A very special time for infant and adult baptisms is during the Easter Vigil Mass, which is held on the Saturday night before Easter Sunday morning. Indeed, unbaptised adults who also wish to become Catholics often receive all three sacraments of initiation: Baptism, Confirmation and the Eucharist, at the same time, during the Easter Vigil Mass.

The Ceremony

1.   THE RECEPTION

The child is presented for baptism by his/her parents. The priest welcomes them and invites them to the baptismal font. Also present are specially chosen *godparents* who promise to help the parents to bring up the child in the Christian faith. The priest blesses the child, tracing the sign of the cross on his/her forehead. This is a *symbol* that the child belongs to and is a gift from God.

An ornate baptismal font in the Orthodox tradition. ➡

2.   THE SCRIPTURES AND THE SERMON

An extract is read from the *New Testament*, usually one of the Gospel accounts of Jesus' baptism or Jesus' conversation with Nicodemus (see *John* 3:1-21). Then, the priest gives a short sermon to explain the meaning of the reading and the importance of baptism in the Christian religion.

3. THE PRAYER OF EXORCISM AND THE FIRST ANOINTING

The priest prays that this child may be rescued from the slavery of sin and pass into the freedom of God. However, the child will still have free will and can deliberately choose to do good or evil when the time comes for him/her to know right from wrong.

The baby is anointed on the chest with the *oil of catechumens*. This oil is a *symbol* of God's grace strengthening him/her to face the life-long struggle to do good and avoid evil.

4. THE BAPTISMAL PROMISES

Obviously, the child is not at a stage where he/she can make any promises. However, the child is being welcomed into a family that *has* declared its faith.

Having blessed the water in the font, the priest invites the parents and godparents to renew *their* faith. He asks them a set of questions and answers and invites them to declare their acceptance of all the basic Christian teachings found in the Apostle's Creed. Then, he asks the parents to make the Christian faith known to the child as he/she grows up.

5. THE BAPTISM

At this point, water is poured three times over the baby's head as the priest says the following words:

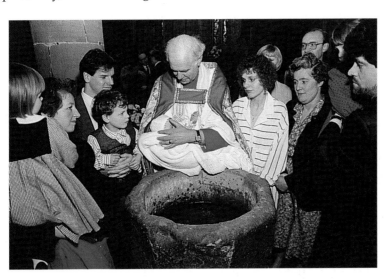

[Child's name], *I baptise you in the name of the Father, and of the Son, and of the Holy Spirit. Amen.*

Water is a very powerful *symbol*. Water gives life but it can also cause death. Stormy seas can drown unfortunate sailors. Flood waters can destroy people's homes. But water can also preserve a person's life in the desert. Rain restores life to wilting plants.

In the sacrament of baptism, water is a symbol of death and life. Christians remember the central mystery of their faith – Jesus died on the cross on Good Friday but rose to new life on Easter Sunday.

The water of baptism *symbolises* (i.e. represents) the purifying power of the Holy Spirit, through which the child *shares* in the death of Jesus, in order to rise with Jesus to new life. As Paul wrote to the early Christians:

> *By our Baptism, then, we were buried with him and shared his death, in order that, just as Christ was raised from death by the glorious power of the Father so also we might live a new life.*
> (*Romans* 6:4)

The child is now welcomed as a new member of the Christian community.

6.   THE SECOND ANOINTING

The child is next anointed with the oil of *chrism*, i.e. a mixture of olive oil and a fragrant perfume called balsam. This oil is a *symbol* with a two-fold meaning:

- the child is called to take up the challenge of living according to the teachings of Jesus;
  and

- the child is declared to have a unique dignity and beauty as a daughter or a son of God.

7.   THE CLOTHING IN A WHITE GARMENT

In the early Church, a catechumen was clothed in a white robe to show that he/she was *clothed in Christ* and had begun a new life when baptised. This is still being done today.

The child is wrapped in a white shawl as a *symbol* that he/she shares in the resurrection of Jesus.

8.   THE BAPTISMAL CANDLE

The parents bring with them a candle which is then lit from the large *Paschal* (or *Easter*) *Candle* in the sanctuary. This represents the resurrection of Jesus.

Light is a very important *symbol* in the Christian religion. Jesus once described himself as

> the *Light of the World*.

Light is a symbol of life, goodness and wisdom. *Darkness* is often used as a symbol of death, wickedness and ignorance.

The lighted candle is a reminder to Christians that Jesus' resurrection is their guarantee that death is not the end but a gateway to eternal life with God.

9.   THE LORD'S PRAYER AND FINAL BLESSING

All present then recite the Our Father to indicate that the child is now finally a member of the Christian community and can call God his/her Father. The ceremony concludes with the priest asking for God's blessing on the child's mother, father and all those present.

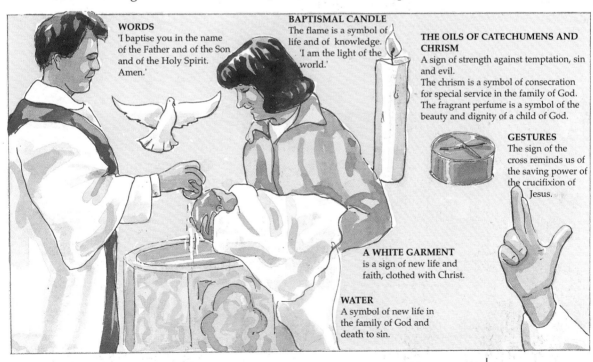

WORDS
'I baptise you in the name of the Father and of the Son and of the Holy Spirit. Amen.'

BAPTISMAL CANDLE
The flame is a symbol of life and of knowledge.
'I am the light of the world.'

THE OILS OF CATECHUMENS AND CHRISM
A sign of strength against temptation, sin and evil.
The chrism is a symbol of consecration for special service in the family of God. The fragrant perfume is a symbol of the beauty and dignity of a child of God.

GESTURES
The sign of the cross reminds us of the saving power of the crucifixion of Jesus.

A WHITE GARMENT
is a sign of new life and faith, clothed with Christ.

WATER
A symbol of new life in the family of God and death to sin.

▲ The symbols of Baptism.

QUESTIONS

1. Match up the explanations in column *B* with the word in column *A*.

A	B
font	candidate for baptism
baptism	person responsible for helping in a child's religious upbringing
catechumen	basin holding water for baptism
godparent	ceremony held to initiate a person into the Christian community

2. Name the Christian denomination that will only baptise adults.
3. Why do both the Catholic tradition and the Orthodox tradition baptise infants?
4. Name the *two* types of oil used in baptism. Explain what each symbolises (i.e. represents).
5. Why are the parents and godparents asked to declare their acceptance of all the basic Christian teachings found in the Apostle's Creed?
6. Explain the use of the following symbols in baptism:
   ■ *water*   ■ *the lighted candle*   ■ *the white shawl*
7. What is the role of the godparent in the ceremony of baptism?

JOURNAL WORK

Suppose you are asked to be a godparent. Write down three things you could do to help in a child's religious upbringing.

What kind of problems might you encounter in fulfilling the role of godparent?

Confirmation

Meaning

Confirmation is also a sacrament of initiation. Like baptism, it may be received only *once*.

The word *confirmation* comes from the Latin word *confirmare* meaning *to strengthen*. This sacrament *strengthens* baptised Christians and through the power of the Holy Spirit helps them as they try to be active, caring followers of Jesus Christ.

History

In the early days of Christianity, when most converts were adults, Christians were usually baptised and confirmed during the *same* ceremony. As Christianity grew and gained new members, however, adult converts as well as infants and children were baptised by priests and *later* confirmed by bishops in a *separate* ceremony.

Since the Middle Ages, the Catholic Church has offered the sacrament of confirmation to young Catholics who are just entering their teenage years. In the Orthodox tradition, however, people are *still* baptised and confirmed in the same ceremony.

The Ceremony

The ceremony of confirmation in the Catholic Church is in four parts:

1. THE PRESENTATION OF THE CANDIDATE

The candidate for confirmation normally receives this sacrament during a specially held Mass. Confirmation is usually given by a bishop. He completes or confirms the process of initiation into the Christian community begun at baptism.

2. THE RENEWAL OF BAPTISMAL VOWS

Most Catholics are baptised when they are babies. At that time, they were incapable of understanding what it means to be a Christian. By the time they are presented for the sacrament of confirmation they are considered to be old enough to understand how challenging it is to follow Jesus' teachings. They are thought to be ready to make the promises made on their behalf at baptism, their *own*.

The candidate for confirmation publicly

■ rejects all that is evil
   and

■ declares belief in the main teachings of the Catholic Church regarding the Trinity, the communion of saints, the forgiveness of sins, the resurrection of the body, and the life everlasting.

3. THE LAYING ON OF HANDS

The bishop lays his hands on the head of each person to be confirmed. This is a gesture dating back to ancient times. It asked for God's grace to strengthen a person to face a special task.

In the sacrament of confirmation, each candidate receives his/her *vocation* (from the Latin Word *vocare* meaning *to call*). The bishop calls on them to be witnesses to the values of Jesus Christ, i.e. to be courageous, active, forgiving, generous and positive.

The bishop reminds them that the Holy Spirit will strengthen them to be true followers of Jesus Christ, just as the disciples were strengthened on the first Pentecost.

Then the bishop prays that the candidates for confirmation will receive the seven gifts of the Holy Spirit. They are:

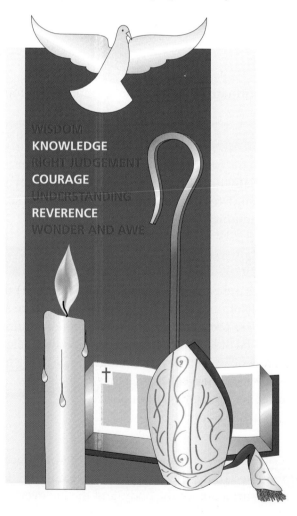

WISDOM
KNOWLEDGE
RIGHT JUDGEMENT
COURAGE
UNDERSTANDING
REVERENCE
WONDER AND AWE

1. *Wisdom*   –   seeing the world and people as Jesus sees them.

2. *Understanding*   –   realising how to love God and other people.

3. *Right Judgment* –   knowing what is the right thing to do in difficult situations.

4. *Courage*   –   doing what is right despite opposition.

5. *Knowledge*   –   knowing and loving God – the answer to all life's great mysteries.

6. *Reverence*   –   taking time and care to pray and worship.

7. *Wonder and Awe* –   being aware of the great goodness of God and realising that, despite our selfishness and weakness, God loves us (see *Galatians* 5:22-25).

4.   THE ANOINTING WITH CHRISM

The bishop makes the sign of the cross on each candidate's forehead with the holy oil of chrism and says

> [Name], *be sealed with the gift of the Holy Spirit.*

Oil, as we have seen, is an important Christian symbol. Oil has healing qualities (see *Luke* 10:34). It is also used to strengthen athletes and make them supple in preparation for a contest.

In the confirmation ceremony, oil symbolises (i.e. represents) how the power of the Holy Spirit strengthens a Christian in his/her commitment to follow the teachings of Jesus Christ.

The sacrament of confirmation. ➡

QUESTIONS

1. What is the origin of the word *confirmation*?
2. Explain the *purpose* of the sacrament of confirmation.
3. In what way does the Orthodox Church differ from the Catholic Church regarding the sacrament of confirmation?
4. By *whom* is the sacrament of confirmation usually given?
5. Explain the meaning of the word *vocation*.
6. What is a person being confirmed *called upon* to do?
7. Match the description of the seven gifts in column *B* with the name of each gift in column *A*.

A GIFT	B MEANING
Wisdom	Knowing what is the right thing to do in difficult situations.
Understanding	Knowing and loving God – the answer to all life's great mysteries.
Right Judgment	Taking time and care to pray and worship.
Courage	Being aware of the great goodness of God and realising that, despite our selfishness and weakness, God loves us.
Knowledge	Doing what we know is right despite opposition.
Reverence	Seeing the world and people as Jesus sees them.
Wonder and Awe	Realising how to love God and other people.

8. What does the oil of chrism *symbolise* in the confirmation ceremony?

JOURNAL WORK

Design a poster illustrating the seven gifts of the Holy Spirit.

CHAPTER SIXTEEN

SACRAMENTS OF INITIATION II: THE EUCHARIST

Names

The word *eucharist* comes from the Greek word *eucharistia* which means *thanksgiving*. Indeed, the sacrament of the eucharist is essentially a celebration of the *Paschal Mystery* (i.e. Jesus' death and resurrection) which takes place in the context of praise and thanksgiving for all God has done and continues to do for human beings.

The sacrament of the eucharist is *the* central ritual of the *liturgy* (i.e. the official public worship) of the Catholic Church. It is celebrated every day, but above all on Sunday, the first day of the week, because it is the day of Jesus' resurrection. Catholics are expected to be fully informed about the Mass, to take part in it with devotion and to live out its message in daily life.

When Catholics talk about the sacrament of the eucharist, they often simply refer to it as *the Mass*. This is the name that it has had since the sixth or seventh century. The word *mass* comes from the Latin word *missio* meaning *the sending*. This refers to the final words of the mass when said in Latin: *Ite missa est*. This means *Go, you are sent*.

The Last Supper by Poussin. ▼

Order of the Mass

The basic elements and overall structure of the Mass were settled upon as early as the second century A.D. The Mass consists of *four* sections.

INTRODUCTORY RITES

This consists of
- Entrance Procession
- Greeting
- Penitential Rite (i.e. confession of sins)
- Kyrie
- (Gloria)
- Opening Prayer

The purpose of these rites is to help the assembled people to become a *worshipping community* of people united in faith, and to prepare them for listening to God's word and celebrating the eucharist.

Unlike the first disciples, today's Christians do not have the privilege of seeing the risen Jesus with their own eyes or touching his wounds (see *John* 20:24-29). However, modern Christians can draw encouragement and inspiration from the story of the two disappointed and dismayed disciples who encountered the risen Jesus on the road to Emmaus (see *Luke* 24:13-35).

Catholics believe that what happened on the road to Emmaus and during the meal afterwards is what takes place each time they gather to celebrate Mass. They believe that they *encounter* the risen Jesus in *three* ways:

- in the sacred scriptures
- in the breaking of bread
- in other people.

LITURGY OF THE WORD

This consists of
- First Reading (*Old Testament*)
- Responsorial Psalm
- Second Reading (*New Testament*)
- Gospel
    Gospel Acclamation
    Proclamation of the Gospel
- Homily (i.e. sermon)
- Creed (usually *Nicene*)
- Prayers of the Faithful

In the Liturgy of the Word, Catholics are expected to listen to the Word of God with the same attentiveness of mind and openness of heart as the two disciples on the road to Emmaus showed as Jesus explained the scriptures to them.

Jesus speaks to his followers today when the scriptures are read at Mass. Ideally, the homily following the scripture readings will explain their meaning and show how their messages can be applied in daily life.

LITURGY OF THE EUCHARIST

This consists of
- Presentation of Gifts
- Eucharistic Prayer and *Consecration* i.e. where the bread and wine become the body and blood of Jesus Christ
- Our Father
- Rite of Peace
- Communion

In the Liturgy of the Eucharist, when the bishop or priest breaks and blesses the bread, Jesus is *really* and *truly present* to people, just as he was present to the disciples in the breaking of the bread on the first Easter Sunday evening (see *Luke* 24:30-31).

When Catholics receive the *sacred host* at communion, they are receiving the gift of the living Jesus himself to *nourish* their faith and *strengthen* them to follow his way.

CONCLUDING RITES

This consists of
- Final Blessing in the name of the Trinity
- Dismissal (i.e. sending out) in the *peace* of Christ to love one another.

When the disciples met Jesus on the road to Emmaus, they did *not* recognise him at first. Only later did they realise that this stranger was actually Jesus.

Christians today are called to see the face of Jesus in others. They are challenged to go out and show their love for God in the way they treat people in everyday situations. They must recognise that Jesus is there wherever they look, in the faces of famine victims, frightened refugees, homeless people, and those suffering from AIDS-related illnesses.

But Christians are called not only to recognise the needs of others. They must also *respond* positively to them.

Like the first disciples, today's Christians are called not only to believe that Jesus has risen, but to show how this makes a difference in their lives. This is a great challenge.

The Mass.

1 Greeting, Penitential Rite

6 Our Father, Sign of Peace

2 Liturgy of the Word

7 Communion

3 Creed, Prayers

4 Offertory

5 Preface, Eucharistic Prayer

8 Blessing
'Go in peace to love and serve the Lord.'

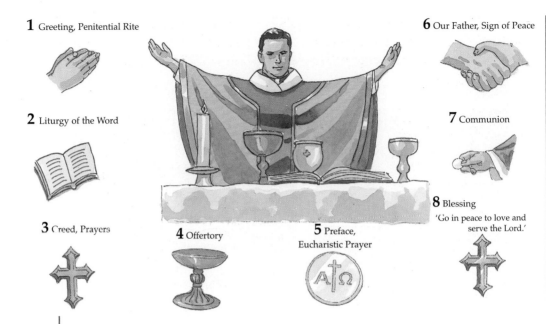

Differences

Since the Reformation of the sixteenth century, major differences have existed between Catholics and Protestants over the meaning of the eucharist.

Though many *Protestants* celebrate the eucharist, some do *not*, notably the Society of Friends and the Salvation Army. Those Protestants who do celebrate the eucharist differ in the frequency of celebration. For example, whereas the Church of Ireland celebrates the eucharist on the first and third Sundays of every month, the Presbyterian Church only holds a communion service once or twice a year. Indeed, the Presbyterian and the Methodist Churches largely emphasise listening to scripture readings and to the preacher's words of explanation and guidance as their regular form of Sunday worship.

Many Protestants who do celebrate the eucharist refer to it as *the Lord's Supper*. They do so to emphasise their belief that:

- The eucharist is simply a meal eaten in memory of Jesus' life, death and resurrection.
- Nothing happens to the bread and the wine during the eucharistic prayer. There is no mysterious change in them after they have been blessed.
- The bread and wine are *purely* symbols which serve to remind Christians of the presence of the risen Jesus in his people, and nothing more.

In contrast, *Catholics* believe that at the moment of consecration during the Liturgy of the Eucharist:

- A real change *does* occur in the bread and wine offered.

■ Through the words and actions of a bishop or a priest, and the invocation of the Holy Spirit, the bread ceases to be bread and becomes the *body* of Jesus, and the wine ceases to be wine and becomes the *blood* of Jesus.

■ There has been no change in the *outer* appearances of the bread and the wine. They still look and taste the same. However, their *inner* reality has been *transformed* through the power of God. The risen Jesus is *truly* and *fully present* under the form of bread and wine on the altar.

■ These three points form what is called the doctrine of *transubstantiation*.

QUESTIONS

1. Explain the origin of the word *eucharist*.
2. What is the *Paschal Mystery*?
3. Why is Sunday *the* special day of worship for Catholics?
4. Explain the origin of the word *mass*.
5. What are the *four* sections of the Mass?
6. State the *three* ways in which Catholics believe that they can *encounter* or recognise the presence of the risen Jesus in today's world.
7. What kind of action is a Catholic expected to undertake when he/she is *sent out* at the end of the mass?
8. Which Protestant Churches do not celebrate the eucharist?
9. Why do many Protestant Christians refer to the celebration of the eucharist as *the Lord's Supper*?
10. What is meant by the Catholic doctrine of *transubstantiation*?

Aspects of the Mass

1.   THE MASS AS SACRIFICE

Sacrifice is the word used to describe *anything of value offered to God in worship.*

Until the destruction of Jerusalem by the Romans in A.D. 70, the Jews offered sacrifices to God in the Temple. A sacrifice was usually an animal or a bird. In the case of the Jewish feast of Passover, a lamb was sacrificed.

During the eucharistic prayer Jesus is referred to as *the Lamb of God.* This is because the Mass has its roots in the Jewish Passover meal which commemorates the delivery of the Hebrews from slavery in Egypt.

The story of the first Passover is told in the book of *Exodus.* In order to persuade the reluctant pharaoh to let the Hebrews go free, God sent a series of warnings, each of which the pharaoh ignored. Finally, God sent the angel of death to kill every first-born son of Egypt.

During the first Passover, every Jewish household was instructed to sacrifice a lamb and sprinkle its blood on their door posts so that the angel of death would see the blood and *pass over* them, sparing the life of their first-born son.

When Jesus referred to himself as the *Lamb of God*, and the bread and wine of the Last Supper as his body and blood, he was speaking of himself as the *new* Passover sacrifice.

The Synoptic Gospels recount, how on Holy Thursday evening Jesus gathered his disciples around him, then

> *He took a piece of bread, gave thanks to God, broke it, and gave it to them saying 'This is my body, which is given for you. Do this in memory of me.'*
> *Luke* 22:19

This action of Jesus pointed to the breaking of his body on the cross the very next day.

Then, in the same way, Jesus

> *gave them the cup after the supper, saying 'This cup is God's new covenant (i.e. agreement) sealed with my blood, which is poured out for you.'*
> *Luke* 22:20

When Jesus did this, he pointed to the shedding of his blood at his scourging and crucifixion the following day.

Jesus identified himself as the *new* Lamb, as the perfect sacrifice whose blood would be shed, whose body would be broken and whose life would be given so that *all* people might be set *free* from slavery to *sin* (i.e. selfishness and wrongdoing). The Mass is the *new* and perfect Passover.

The Mass, however, does *more* than simply recall Jesus' sacrifice on Good Friday.

> *In the eucharist, Christ gives the very body which he gave up for us on the cross, the very blood which he 'poured out for many for the forgiveness of sins'. The eucharist is thus a sacrifice because it re-presents (makes present) the sacrifice of the cross.*
> – Catechism of the Catholic Church (1365 – 1366).

The Catholic Church teaches that:

■ The sacrifice of Jesus on the cross and the sacrifice of the Eucharist are one single sacrifice. The same Christ, offered on Calvary, is offered in the Mass.

■ Jesus' sacrifice is *not* only something that happened in the past that people remember. The Mass is *more* than a memorial service. It calls to mind and brings about a *present* reality.

Although Jesus' death is *over* once and for all, his gift of himself to us goes on today. Jesus is really *present* in the Mass, just as he was to the disciples at Emmaus two thousand years ago.

■ The sacrifice of Jesus is an event that becomes *one* with people's own experience of life in the here and now. In the Mass, the worshipping community is *transformed* into the *body of Christ* in the world today. They are called to live Jesus' way and are strengthened to work towards the fulfilment of God's plan for the world.

■ The Mass invites those who participate in it to *unite* their own lives and sufferings with Jesus' passion and death. For if those present at the celebration of the eucharist are united with Jesus in his death, then they are *also* united with him in his *rising* to new life.

Thus the Mass points forward to a *future* reunion with Jesus in heaven, where those who have faithfully followed his way will be rewarded with lives full of peace, joy and contentment for all eternity.

The Body of Christ.
➡

2. THE MASS AS CELEBRATION OF UNITY AND THANKSGIVING

Eating and drinking together is one of the most sociable things that people can do. When a family or group of friends share a meal, there is an experience of *unity* among them.

The Mass has its origins in the words and actions of Jesus at the last supper he shared with his disciples. All those present at the Mass are united in thanksgiving for the good things God has done and continues to do for them through Jesus Christ. Furthermore, when Catholics share the eucharist it signifies the unity, not just between those present at a particular Mass, but between *all members* of the entire Catholic community worldwide.

For Catholics, going to Mass and receiving communion is at the very centre of their lives as Christians. The eucharist is the realisation of God's vision of how people should live and relate to one another:

■ All people are invited to gather as one community around the altar, united by the presence of Jesus, who promised that:

Where two or three are gathered in my name there I will be in the midst of them.

■ People are called to be willing to forgive and make peace, to be ready to encourage and share generously with one another – even going so far as being ready to lay down their lives for one another.

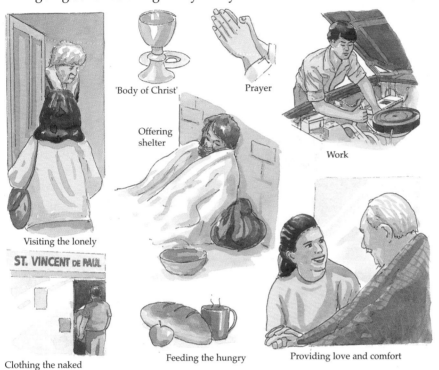

'Body of Christ'

Prayer

Offering shelter

Work

Visiting the lonely

ST. VINCENT DE PAUL

Clothing the naked

Feeding the hungry

Providing love and comfort

'Go in peace to love and serve the Lord'.

QUESTIONS

1. What is the meaning of the word *sacrifice*?
2. Why is Jesus referred to as *the Lamb of God* during the Eucharistic prayer?
3. What was the meaning of Jesus (a) breaking the bread and (b) pouring out wine with his disciples on Holy Thursday evening?
4. Why is the Mass called the *new Passover*?
5. In what ways does the Mass point to events in:
   (a) the past
   (b) the present
   (c) the future?
6. What kind of *Unity* does sharing in the eucharist signify for Catholics?

Involvement

▲
Celebrating the eucharist.

Many forms of entertainment, such as cinema or television simply ask people to sit back, relax and enjoy the experience. They *make no demands* on people and ask them to be *passive* observers rather than *active* participants.

The eucharist is *the focal point* of the whole Christian life for Catholics. Catholics are called to be active participants in the celebration of the eucharist, *not* passive spectators.

It is true that only a bishop or a priest can *preside* at a Mass (i.e. lead the congregation in worship) and *consecrate* the bread and wine. However, the Mass is essentially a *communal* act of worship, i.e. all those people gathered in Christ's name share in the celebration of the Eucharist.

The members of a congregation can actively participate in the Mass in a number of ways:

1.   LISTENING

If you respect someone, you show this by paying attention when he/she is speaking to you. Such *active listening* is an essential part of any relationship between people who care about one another.

Catholics are expected to listen attentively to the readings and prayers at Mass. Not merely out of courtesy to the person speaking, but because he/she is drawing their attention to the *source* of this Good News – *God*.

People can use their imaginations to bring Bible stories to life. They can imagine what it would have been like to witness some important event in the life of Jesus. They can reflect on the meaning of a reading or prayer, make its teaching their own and apply it to their situation.

2.   RECITING

At various moments in the Mass, the congregation is asked to *recite* certain prayers, such as the Our Father, or to *respond* to others, as in the Prayers of the Faithful. People should do so consciously, i.e. reflecting on the meaning of the prayer.

3.   GESTURING

As we stated earlier, gestures are *symbols* that we perform.

When people reflect upon the *meaning* of certain gestures and *consciously* perform them, then they are participating in the celebration of the eucharist.

For example:

- *Kneeling* — This acknowledges the greatness of God, who alone is to be worshipped.

- *Standing* — This recalls Jesus' rising from the dead on Easter Sunday.

- *Blessing* — By making the sign of the cross, a person identifies him/herself as a follower of Jesus Christ.

- *Shaking hands* — This *sign of peace* should reveal a genuine desire to be a peacemaker and source of help and encouragement to those one encounters in everyday situations.

4.   COMMUNION

Full participation in the sacrament of the eucharist involves receiving *communion*, i.e. consuming the body of Jesus under the form of bread and, on occasion, his blood in the form of wine. Jesus is really present in the eucharist. When Catholics receive his body and blood they are receiving spiritual nourishment to sustain them in their faith in, and commitment to, Jesus.

Before receiving communion, Catholics should first ask to be purified from *sin* (i.e. selfishness and wrongdoing). A Catholic who has committed a *grave* (i.e. very serious) sin should go to *confession* and receive God's forgiveness. However, all those present at the Mass participate in the *penitential rite* at the beginning of the ceremony, which purifies them from less serious sins.

Catholics are also expected to fast – no food or liquids (besides water), may be taken within one hour prior to receiving communion.

5.   MINISTRY

Members of the community may participate in a special way in the celebration of the eucharist, by volunteering to help in the following *roles*:

- readers
- altar servers
- choir members
- musicians
- eucharistic ministers (i.e. distributors of holy communion).

QUESTIONS

1. Who are the only people permitted to preside at the Mass and who alone can consecrate the bread and wine?
2. The Mass is described as *essentially a communal act*. What does this mean?
3. List the *five* ways in which a member of a Catholic congregation can *participate* in the Mass.
4. What is meant by *active listening* to the scriptures?
5. Explain the meaning of the following gestures:
   - *kneeling*
   - *standing*
   - *blessing*
   - *shaking hands*.
6. What is meant by *receiving communion*?
7. How should a Catholic prepare for receiving communion?
8. List *five roles* for which a member of a Catholic congregation can volunteer to help in the celebration of the eucharist.

JOURNAL WORK

Hymn singing is a very important part in all Christian worship. John and Charles Wesley wrote some famous hymns. When asked why they had done so, they replied that they wanted *to inject some life into services.*

(a) What do you think they meant by this answer?

(b) How important do you think music is to the celebration of the eucharist?

CHAPTER SEVENTEEN

CHRISTIAN PILGRIMAGE

Introduction

The word *pilgrim* comes from the Latin *peregrinus* meaning *foreign*, i.e. a stranger passing through one's land on his/her way to a much-desired destination. The early Christians understood themselves as a *pilgrim people* on a *journey* through this world. They believed that they were following a route already mapped out for them by Jesus. He had assured them that he was

> *the Way, the Truth and the Life.*
> John 14:6.

If they stayed on course, by remaining faithful to Jesus, then they would reach their destination – the joy of sharing eternal life with God.

Since earliest times, Christians have gone on *pilgrimages*, i.e. journeys to places of religious importance. They have done this to remind themselves that life itself is a great journey. Where that journey ends is decided by the way they live their lives.

A pilgrimage can be undertaken either by one person travelling alone or by a guided group travelling together.

▲ Life is a pilgrimage.

Pilgrimage Sites

During the Middle Ages, pilgrimages became very popular. The main pilgrimage sites of that period are shown in the map below.

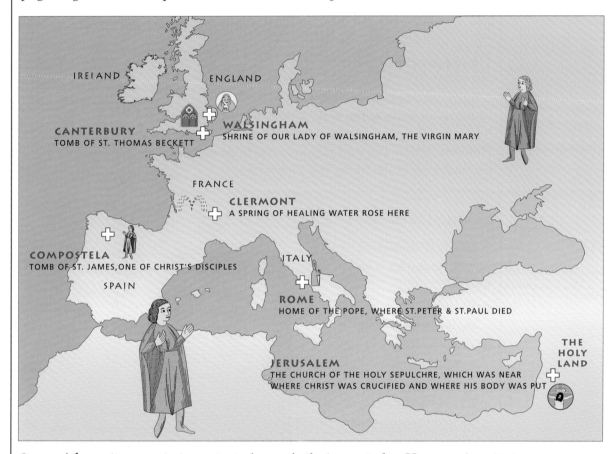

IRELAND

ENGLAND

CANTERBURY
TOMB OF ST. THOMAS BECKETT

WALSINGHAM
SHRINE OF OUR LADY OF WALSINGHAM, THE VIRGIN MARY

FRANCE

CLERMONT
A SPRING OF HEALING WATER ROSE HERE

COMPOSTELA
TOMB OF ST. JAMES, ONE OF CHRIST'S DISCIPLES

SPAIN

ITALY

ROME
HOME OF THE POPE, WHERE ST.PETER & ST.PAUL DIED

JERUSALEM
THE CHURCH OF THE HOLY SEPULCHRE, WHICH WAS NEAR WHERE CHRIST WAS CRUCIFIED AND WHERE HIS BODY WAS PUT

THE HOLY LAND

▲
Important Medieval pilgrimage sites.

Some of these sites remain important places of pilgrimage today. However, in the last two centuries, many new Christian pilgrimage sites have developed, especially in places where Mary, the mother of Jesus, is said to have appeared.

A place may become a centre of pilgrimage for one of a number of reasons:

- It may be a place associated with the life of Jesus; e.g. Bethlehem or Jerusalem.

- It may be a place where an *apparition* (i.e. appearance) of Mary is said to have occurred; e.g. Knock or Lourdes.

- It may be a place where a saint (i.e. holy man or holy woman) was buried; e.g. Downpatrick, which is the site of St Patrick's tomb.

- It may be a place connected with important events in the life of a saint; e.g. *Croagh Patrick* where St Patrick is believed to have fasted and prayed in his desire to grow close to God.

It is important to remember that, while Christians go to such places expecting to meet God in a special way, God is *not* only present in these *official* holy sites. Christians believe that God is *everywhere* in life.

When Christians give a certain place a special religious status by referring to it as *holy ground*, they do so to remind themselves that all of the world is holy ground. It is a gift from God that should be treated with *respect*.

Difference

It is *not* compulsory for Christians to go on a pilgrimage. In contrast, all Muslims are expected to make a pilgrimage to Mecca at least once in their lives, though only when they have taken care of their other responsibilities. However, if they can find someone else to go in their place, they may be excused from undertaking this pilgrimage.

Reasons for Pilgrimage

People may undertake to go on pilgrimage for a variety of reasons:

- To seek God's *forgiveness* for sin (i.e. wrongdoing).
- To ask for God's *guidance* before making an important decision.
- To receive the *strength* needed to face a major crisis in life.
- To *strengthen* their faith in God by visiting places connected with the life of Jesus.
- To *revitalise* their faith and encourage them to be more committed to living out their religious beliefs.
- To build bonds of *friendship* with fellow pilgrims.

QUESTIONS

1. Explain the origin of the word *pilgrim*.
2. Why did the early Christians see themselves as a *pilgrim people*?
3. What is a *pilgrimage*?
4. Name three important places of pilgrimage in the Middle Ages.
5. For each of the following places, state why it has become a place of pilgrimage
   (a) Knock
   (b) Downpatrick
   (c) Bethlehem
   (d) Croagh Patrick.
6. When Christians refer to some particular place as *holy ground*, of what are they seeking to remind themselves?
7. What do Muslims believe about going on pilgrimage?

JOURNAL WORK

Suggest what you consider to be the main reasons for going on a pilgrimage.

Places of Pilgrimage

The Holy Land

This is the name given by Christians to the land where Jesus' extraordinary story unfolded. Two thousand years ago it was the Roman province of Palestine. Today it is divided among the states of Israel, Palestine, Lebanon, Jordan and Syria.

The Holy Land is probably the most frequently visited pilgrimage site for Christians today. Christians are attracted there by the opportunity to retrace the footsteps of Jesus, on his journey from Galilee to his death and resurrection in Jerusalem.

The three main sites are:

■ *Bethlehem*
This is where the Church of the Nativity stands on what is thought to be the site of Jesus' birth.

■ *Nazareth*
Here the Basilica of the Annunciation and the Church of St Gabriel were built to commemorate the angel's message that Mary had been chosen to be the mother of the Messiah.

■ *Jerusalem*

This is the principal centre of pilgrimage for Christians, particularly during Easter. The main focus of a pilgrimage is usually the *Via Dolorosa* (i.e. *the Street of Sorrows* or *the Way of Grief*). This is the route that Jesus took as he carried his cross from Pilate's residence to his place of execution outside the city walls, and from there to his place of burial.

▲ The Via Dolorosa on Good Friday.

Since the Middle Ages, pilgrims have stopped at fourteen points along the *Via Dolorosa* for readings, prayers and reflection. Eventually this pilgrim ritual formed the basis for what became known as the *Stations of the Cross* (see box).

At the end of the *Via Dolorosa* is the Church of the Holy Sepulchre, which contains the site of Jesus' crucifixion and the tomb where he was buried. Helena, the mother of the first Christian emperor of Rome, Constantine, had a church built on this site after she had made her first pilgrimage to the Holy Land in A.D. 326. This church is crammed to capacity for Mass on Easter morning, when Christians celebrate the resurrection of Jesus.

THE STATIONS OF THE CROSS

These are generally found on the walls of Catholic churches. Each marks a stage of Jesus' suffering on Good Friday.

1. Jesus is condemned to death by Pilate.
   Matthew 27:15-26; Mark 15:6-15; Luke 23:17-15

2. Jesus receives his cross.
   John 19:17

THE STATIONS OF THE CROSS

3. Jesus falls beneath the cross for the first time.

4. Jesus meets his mother.

5. Simon of Cyrene helps Jesus to carry the cross.
   Matthew 27:32; Mark 15:21; Luke 23:26

6. Veronica wipes the face of Jesus.

7. Jesus falls a second time.

8. Jesus comforts the women of Jerusalem.
   Luke 23:27-31

9. Jesus falls a third time.

10. Jesus is stripped and offered a sponge soaked with bitter wine.
    Matthew 27:28-31, 33-4; Mark 15:16-20

11. Jesus is nailed to the cross, between two thieves.
    Matthew 27:33; Mark 15:24; Luke 23:33

12. Jesus dies on the cross.
    Matthew 27:45-56; Mark 15:33-41; Luke 23:44-9; John 19:28-30

13. Jesus is taken down from the cross and laid in his mother's arms.
    This scene is depicted by Michelangelo in his *Pieta*.

14. Jesus is placed in the tomb.
    Matthew 27:57-61; Mark 15:42-7; Luke 23:50-56; John 19:31-42

N.B.

Some of the incidents mentioned in the Stations of the Cross were not recorded in the Gospel accounts. They were included, however, to emphasis the great suffering Jesus experienced.

Christians who have been unable to go to Jerusalem and follow the *Via Dolorosa*, have been able to follow the footsteps of Jesus in their local church. By moving around the church and stopping to pray at each station, they have been able to make their own short pilgrimage.

Rome

Rome has been an important centre of pilgrimage for over one thousand six hundred years. It is the place where both Peter and Paul were executed on the orders of the Emperor Nero. Peter was the first leader of the Christian

▲ St Peter's Basilica, Rome.

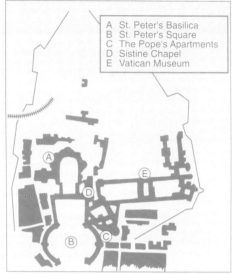

▲ Diagram of the Vatican City State.

community. His successors, who were given the title *pope*, have resided in Rome, except for a few brief periods in exile, ever since.

The headquarters of the Catholic Church is located in the *Vatican*, an independent city state, situated in the heart of Rome. Huge crowds flock to the Vatican to attend one of the pope's regular public audiences and to receive his blessing.

The city of Rome's many historic churches are packed with pilgrims during the most important religious feasts of the Christian calendar – Easter and Christmas.

Two sites in particular draw large numbers of pilgrims:

- *St Peter's Basilica* (i.e. *great church*) which was built on the site of Peter's tomb.

- *The Church of St Paul outside the Walls* which was built on the site of Paul's tomb.

QUESTIONS

1. Where can the following places of pilgrimage be found:
   (a) The Basilica of the Annunciation
   (b) The Church of St Paul outside the Walls
   (c) The Church of the Holy Sepulchre
   (d) St Peter's Basilica
   (e) The Church of the Nativity?

QUESTIONS CONTD

2. What is the meaning of the street name *Via Dolorosa*?
3. Why are certain incidents *not* recorded in the Gospels, included in the Stations of the Cross?
4. Which Station of the Cross was depicted by Michelangelo in his *Pieta*?
5. Where is the headquarters of the Catholic Church located?
6. Which important Christian saints were martyred and buried in Rome?

Croagh Patrick

Croagh Patrick in County Mayo has been a popular place of pilgrimage for Irish people since the Middle Ages. As early as 1113, it was reported that a thunderbolt struck the mountain killing thirty fasting pilgrims.

Most pilgrimages involve putting up with some kind of hardship. In the case of Croagh Patrick, it is climbing the mountain.

Croagh Patrick is high by Irish standards, rising some seven hundred and sixty-five metres above the surrounding countryside. The path to the top is four kilometres long. Near the top it is steep and covered with loose rock.

In the past, pilgrimages were always made in one's bare feet. This was considered an act of humility. Although it is no longer felt to be so necessary, some people still climb the mountain in their bare feet to show their sorrow for the ways they have offended God.

Pilgrims climb Croagh Patrick in order to walk where Patrick walked, to kneel where he knelt down and to pray where he prayed. Going on pilgrimage is an act of *devotion* to God.

Pilgrim at prayer.

Lourdes

Lourdes in south-west France only became a place of pilgrimage in the nineteenth century. On 11 February 1858, a fourteen-year-old girl named

Bernadette Soubirous had the first of a series of visions of the Blessed Virgin Mary, the Mother of Jesus. They took place in a little grotto outside the town and occurred on eighteen occasions over a period of six months.

During the ninth apparition, Mary told Bernadette to dig at a certain place in the grotto. From there a spring of water emerged. Ever since then there have been stories of miraculous healings associated with this spring. Not surprisingly, many Catholics journey to Lourdes in search of healing. Several million people visit Lourdes each year.

Each evening during the pilgrimage season, thousands

▲ Pilgrimage at Lourdes, 1936.

of pilgrims take part in a torchlit procession through the streets of Lourdes. Prayers and hymns are relayed over loudspeakers. Those who cannot walk are pushed through the streets in wheelchairs by volunteer helpers.

The highlight of the pilgrimage is the visit to the grotto to bathe in its waters. Many pilgrims have claimed that they were healed after visiting Lourdes. Of the reported five thousand cures, however, only *fifty-eight* have been declared miraculous by Catholic Church authorities.

Anyone who claims that he/she has been healed after visiting Lourdes is asked to undergo a series of medical investigations conducted by independent experts. Before deciding if a cure is miraculous, Catholic Church authorities ask a number of questions:

■ Was the disease serious?

■ Was the cure sudden and unexpected?

■ Is it a complete cure?

■ Has it lasted at least three years?

■ Was it achieved without any medical treatment?

■ Has the cure been proven by medical investigation?

If a person can answer *yes* to all of these questions, then the cure is deemed to be *miraculous*, i.e. it can only be explained by God's direct intervention.

Many sick people who have not been physically cured at Lourdes, however, claim that their pilgrimage *was* worthwhile. They often say that it brought them closer to God and gave them the courage and strength needed to cope with their illnesses.

QUESTIONS

1. Why, in the past, were pilgrimages to the summit of Croagh Patrick always made in one's bare feet?
2. Who was Bernadette Soubirous?
3. How many people are estimated to visit Lourdes each year?
4. What happens in Lourdes each evening during the pilgrimage season?
5. What does it mean to say that a cure is *miraculous*?
6. How many miraculous cures have been confirmed by Catholic Church authorities?
7. What do those who have *not* been physically cured often say about their pilgrimage to Lourdes?

JOURNAL WORK

Imagine you have had a round-the-world tour of some Christian pilgrimage sites. Write a letter to a friend recounting your experiences in these different places.

CHAPTER EIGHTEEN

MARY THE MOTHER OF JESUS

Importance

In terms of specifically Catholic places of pilgrimage, about eighty percent are dedicated to Mary, or as Catholics have traditionally called her *Our Lady*. The Catholic Church presents Mary as *the* perfect example of faith in God.

The Virgin and Child.

Although she did not understand exactly how God was at work in her life (see *Luke* 1: 34), nonetheless Mary trusted God completely and agreed to bring the Son of God into the world (see *Luke* 1:38). Through Mary, humanity and divinity were brought together. It was for this reason that the Council of Ephesus (A.D. 431) gave Mary the title *Theotokos* (a Greek word meaning *God bearer* or *Mother of God*).

The Catholic Church teaches that Mary was the *perfect disciple*, who lived a life of total devotion to Jesus. She is the *model* of how Christians today are called to bring the healing and loving presence of God into the world.

Doctrine

Mary's importance has been acknowledged by the Catholic Church in three important *doctrines* (i.e. teachings). All of these emphasise Mary's *closeness* to God – something all Christians hope to one day enjoy.

1. The Virgin Birth

Both Catholics *and* Protestants accept the Virgin Birth. They teach that Jesus was conceived in Mary's womb through the power of the Holy Spirit and born to her while she was still a *virgin* (i.e. she had not had sexual intercourse with a man).

This means that the Christ was born into the world *not* as a result of human effort but as a totally undeserved gift of love from God.

N.B.
However, Catholic teaching about Mary includes two doctrines (i.e. teachings) that most Protestants do not accept. These have been declared *dogmas* of the Catholic Church i.e. *infallible teachings that must be accepted by all Catholics.*

▲ *The Annunciation* by Fra Angelico.

2. The Immaculate Conception

This was proclaimed a dogma of the Catholic Church by Pope Pius IX in 1854.

This means that from the moment of her conception in her mother's womb, Mary was without sin of any kind. She was totally pure of heart, gentle and loving. As a result, Mary was a fit person to be the mother of the Son of God.

3. The Assumption

This was proclaimed a dogma of the Catholic Church by Pope Pius XII in 1950.

This means that, because of her unique role in human history as the mother of Jesus, Mary was *assumed*, i.e. taken bodily from this world, and instantly united with God in heaven.

The Catholic Church does not say whether or not Mary actually died first before her assumption into heaven. Many early Christians believed that Mary was taken directly into heaven before her death because she was so totally good – *full of grace* (i.e. filled with God's love).

Mary gives Catholics hope that one day, all those who have faithfully lived according to the Gospel message, will also share eternal life with Jesus.

QUESTIONS

1. Explain the term *Theotokos*.
2. Why is Mary considered by the Catholic Church to be the perfect disciple of Jesus?
3. Match the doctrine in box *A* with the explanation in box *B*.

A DOCTRINE	B EXPLANATION
The Virgin Birth	From the moment of her conception Mary was without sin of any kind.
The Immaculate Conception	Mary was assumed, i.e. taken bodily into heaven and instantly united with God.
The Assumption	Jesus was conceived in Mary's womb through the power of the Holy Spirit and born to her while she was still a virgin.

4. What is a *dogma*?

JOURNAL WORK

Read the following prayer called the Magnificat or the Song of Mary.

'My soul glorifies the lord and my spirit rejoices in God my Saviour, for he has been mindful of the humble state of his servant.

From now on all generations will call me blessed, for the Mighty One has done great things for me – holy is his name.

His mercy extends to those who fear him, from generation to generation.

He has performed mighty deeds with his arm; he has scattered those who are proud in their inmost thoughts.

He has brought down rulers from their thrones but has lifted up the humble.

He has filled the hungry with good things but has sent the rich away empty.

He has helped his servant Israel, remembering to be merciful to Abraham and his descendants forever, even as he said to our fathers.'

Luke 1:46-55

(a) In what kind of God did Mary believe?
(b) Some writers have tried to portray Mary as a meek and subservient person. Does the Magnificat present her as this kind of person or does it present her as a strong person? Explain your answer.

The Hail Mary

One of the most familiar prayers for Catholics is the *Hail Mary* (from the Latin *Ave Maria*). This beautiful prayer may be divided into two parts as set out below, with an explanation of each part accompanying it.

I
Hail Mary, full of grace,
The Lord is with thee,
Blessed art thou among women,
And blessed is the fruit of thy womb, Jesus.

PRAYER OF PRAISE

This recalls the Annunciation (*Luke* 1:26-38) when the angel Gabriel gave the joyful news to Mary that God was with her and that she would be the mother of the Messiah.

It also recalls the Visitation (*Luke* 1:39-45) when Mary's cousin Elizabeth greeted her and declared the child in Mary's womb *blessed*.

II
Holy Mary, Mother of God,
Pray for us sinners, now
And in the hour of our death.

PRAYER OF PETITION

This calls upon Mary to care for us as she cared for her son, Jesus. We admit that we are sinners (i.e. people who have done wrong). We seek God's mercy and compassion. We ask Mary to be with us each day and to guide us safely to the end of our lives, so that we may share eternal life with God.

This ancient prayer emphasises the deep faith of Mary and calls on Christians to follow her example.

The Rosary

The Rosary has been an important part of Catholic prayer life since the Middle Ages. It consists of the repetition of certain prayers – the Our Father, the Hail Mary and the Glory Be – while one is reflecting on the meaning of key events in the lives of Jesus and Mary.

The Rosary is divided into three main sections, each one containing five *mysteries* or aspects of the Christian story.

The Joyful Mysteries
1. Annunciation (*Luke* 1:26-38)
2. Visitation (*Luke* 1:39-56)
3. Nativity of Jesus (*Luke* 2:1-7)
4. Presentation of Jesus in the Temple (*Luke* 2:22-32)
5. Finding the Child Jesus in the Temple (*Luke* 2:41-52)

The Sorrowful Mysteries
1. Agony in the Garden (*Mark* 14:32-36)
2. Scourging of Jesus (*John* 18:28-38; 19:1)
3. Crowning with Thorns (*John* 19:2-6)
4. Carrying of the Cross (*John* 19:12-16)
5. Crucifixion and Death of Jesus (*Luke* 23:33-34, 39-46)

The Glorious Mysteries
1. Resurrection of Jesus (*Luke* 24:1-6)
2. Ascension of Jesus (*Acts of the Apostles* 1:9-12)
3. Descent of the Holy Spirit at Pentecost (*Acts of the Apostles* 2:1-4)
4. Assumption of Mary (*Song of Songs* 2:8-14)
5. Coronation of Mary as Queen of Heaven (*Revelation* 12:1-6)

Traditionally, Catholics have used a set of prayer beads called *rosary beads* to help them keep track of where they are, by running a bead through their fingers each time a prayer is said.

The Rosary.

QUESTIONS

1. What are the two parts of the *Hail Mary*?
2. What is the *Rosary*?
3. What are the three main sections of the *Rosary*?
4. What are *rosary beads*? How are they used?

Marian Shrines

Each year huge numbers of pilgrims flock to the many *Marian shrines*, i.e. holy places dedicated to Mary. Many of these places have become centres of pilgrimage because it is believed that Mary herself appeared there. Among the most popular are:

- *Guadalupe* in Mexico
- *Czestochova* in Poland
- *Aparecida* in Brazil
- *Lourdes* in France
- *Fatima* in Portugal.

Knock Shrine, Co Mayo. ▼

Ireland has its Marian shrine at *Knock* in County Mayo. In 1879, fifteen local people claimed that the Virgin Mary had appeared to them. After many years of investigation, Catholic Church authorities declared the apparitions to have been genuine. In 1979, Pope John Paul II visited the shrine at Knock and celebrated Mass there.

It must be understood, however, that despite the respect shown for Mary at these shrines, the focus of all prayer is *not* Mary but *Jesus*. The Catholic Church teaches that the purpose of pilgrimage is to guide the pilgrim to closer union with:

> *Jesus Christ, the Saviour, who is the end of every journey and the source of all holiness.*

Further, Catholics are *not* required by the Church to believe in any of the apparitions of Mary as they are not considered to be essential elements of their religion.

QUESTIONS

1. What is a *Marian shrine*?
2. Where is Ireland's Marian shrine?
3. Read the following statement:
   Catholics are devoted to Mary, but they do not worship her.
   What does this mean?
   Who is the focus of all Christian prayer and worship?
4. Are Catholics required by the Church to believe in any of the apparitions of Mary? Why/Why not?

Part Five

World Religions

CHAPTER NINETEEN

HINDUISM

Meaning

The name *Hindu* comes from the *Indus* river. When invading armies from the west arrived at the banks of the Indus, which is located in present-day Pakistan, they simply gave the name Hindu to everything east *beyond* the river.

Hinduism is the most ancient of the major religions. Indeed, Hindus themselves refer to their religion as *sanatana dharma*, which can be translated as *the ancient religion*.

Origins

Many scholars believe that Hinduism was probably founded by one or more unknown *rishis* (i.e. *wisemen*) who lived in northern India around 2000 B.C. It has developed over the centuries since, from the interchange of beliefs and practices of the many different peoples who settled in India.

Sacred Texts

There are many sacred books in Hinduism. All of them are written in *Sanskrit*, the language of ancient India, which is no longer widely spoken and is largely preserved today by scholars. The word *Sanskrit* means *perfect*. Some Hindus still believe that this language was created by the gods themselves.

Among the most important sacred texts are:

▲
The Hindu Temple at
Madurai, India.

1. *The Vedas*

   These are the oldest writings. They contain *mantras* (i.e. hymns and chants) and *brahamanas* (i.e. explanations of these mantras). They also give guidance as to how people should live.

2. *The Upanishads*

   These contain hymns and poems that reflect on the meaning of life, love, suffering and death. They discuss the idea of *reincarnation*, i.e. that human life is an endless cycle of birth, suffering, death and rebirth. Much of Hindu literature is made up of comments and interpretations of them.

3. *The Mahabharata* and *the Ramayana*

   These are two great epic poems. They teach about the importance of courage, honesty and loyalty.

   The *Mahabharata* is the world's *longest* poem. It concerns the struggles of two families over many years and examines the joys and hardships of everyday life.

   Within the *Mahabharata* is a section called the *Bhagavad Gita*. It is the most famous and most popular of all Hindu religious writings. It contains the teaching of the god Krishna to the nobleman Arjuna.

   The *Ramayana* tells the story of how Rama, a prince whose enemies plotted against him, was forced to leave his kingdom and live in exile in a forest. With him went his wife Sita and his brother Lakshmana. Then, Sita was kidnapped by the demon king Ravana.

   In his struggles to rescue Sita, Rama is presented as a model of courage and honour in the face of evil, and as the example Hindus should follow.

   Rama and Lakshmana rescue Sita and defeat Ravana, with the help of the monkey god Hanuman. Rama finally regains his kingdom. This story celebrates the deep love a husband and a wife should have for each other, and the importance of true friendship.

▲ Using the magic snake, *Shesha*, *Vishnu* orders demons and gods to stir the ocean to keep the world in harmony.

These Hindu religious writings have profoundly shaped Indian art and life.

QUESTIONS

1. Explain the origin of the name *Hinduism*.
2. By what name do Hindus refer to their religion? What does it mean?
3. Who founded Hinduism?
4. When did it begin?
5. What is *Sanskrit*? What does the word mean?
6. What is a *mantra*?
7. Name the oldest Hindu text.
8. What is the title of the most popular of all Hindu religious writings?
9. Who is the hero of the *Ramayana*? Why is he said to set an important example for Hindus?

Brahman

Hindus can be described as *polytheists* because they believe that there are many different gods. Indeed, Hindus are free to worship any god or goddess of their choice. Some three hundred million different gods have been catalogued by scholars. However, the three main gods of Hinduism are *Brahma* (the Creator), *Vishnu* (the Preserver) and *Shiva* (the Destroyer).

Each god fulfils a different role. For example:

■ Whenever evil threatens to take over the world, *Vishnu* is said to come to Earth to fight against it and to restore divine order. Each time he has come as a different being, called an *avatar* (meaning '*one who descends*'). It is believed that he has visited Earth on nine occasions and that Vishnu will make his tenth and final visit at the end of this world.

   Two of Vishnu's best-loved avatars are *Rama* and *Krishna*. There are thousands of Hindu temples dedicated to them.

■ Hindus believe that the universe itself goes through a cycle of birth, growth, destruction and rebirth. *Shiva* is the god who occasionally destroys the universe in order for it to be born again.

   Shiva is presented as a frightening god who is capable of unleashing great destructive power at any time.

However, Hindus believe that these different gods are only pointers towards something much greater and more mysterious that is *beyond* them.

Hinduism teaches that all the gods, and indeed everything in the universe, emanate or flow out from one mysterious, supreme source of all life. They call this *Brahman*.

The Hindu gods. ➡

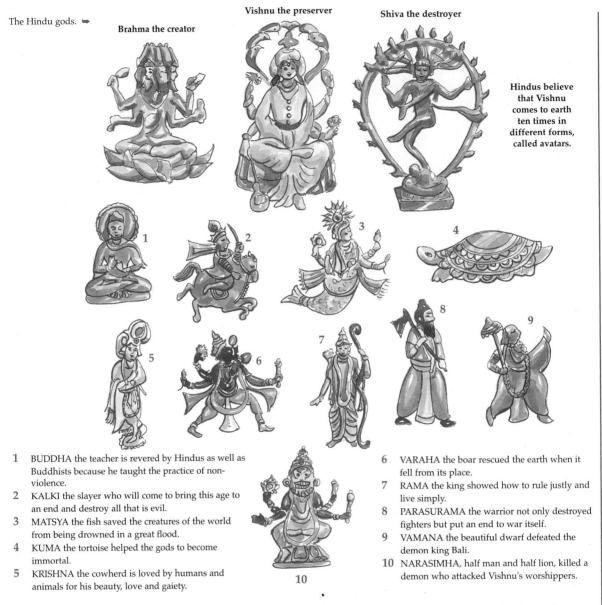

Brahma the creator

Vishnu the preserver

Shiva the destroyer

Hindus believe that Vishnu comes to earth ten times in different forms, called avatars.

1   BUDDHA the teacher is revered by Hindus as well as Buddhists because he taught the practice of non-violence.
2   KALKI the slayer who will come to bring this age to an end and destroy all that is evil.
3   MATSYA the fish saved the creatures of the world from being drowned in a great flood.
4   KUMA the tortoise helped the gods to become immortal.
5   KRISHNA the cowherd is loved by humans and animals for his beauty, love and gaiety.
6   VARAHA the boar rescued the earth when it fell from its place.
7   RAMA the king showed how to rule justly and live simply.
8   PARASURAMA the warrior not only destroyed fighters but put an end to war itself.
9   VAMANA the beautiful dwarf defeated the demon king Bali.
10 NARASIMHA, half man and half lion, killed a demon who attacked Vishnu's worshippers.

Hindus believe that Brahman contains every characteristic of life in the universe: it is both male and female, beautiful and ugly, creative and destructive, all and nothing.

It is important to note, however, that Hindus do *not* believe that Brahman is a person. Brahman is *impersonal*.

Hindu scholars state that it is beyond our human ability to ever fully express what Brahman is in words. It was for this reason that the gods were created to express Brahman's different characteristics.

Genuinely wise people are those who see beyond the different gods to realise that they are merely different ways in which Brahman is expressed.

That which is one, the wise call by many names.
Source : *Rig Veda.*

Hindus believe that the apparent separateness of all things in our world is only an *illusion*. Individuality does *not* really exist. Hindus claim that people, animals, insects, plants, rocks and rivers are merely different aspects of the same thing. They are all merely expressions of the one great *cosmic force* called Brahman.

As one Hindu holy book puts it:

> *I am the taste in the water,*
> *the radiance in the sun and moon …*
> *I am the sound in space, I am*
> *the strength in humanity. I am*
> *the sweet fragrance in the earth.*
> *I am the brilliance in fire.*
> *I am the life in all beings.*
> Source : *Bhagavad Gita.*

▲
The Aum – the symbol of Hinduism.

Brahman is *in* all things and all things *are* Brahman. This belief in the total *oneness* of the universe is called *monism*.

QUESTIONS

1. How many different Hindu gods have been catalogued?
2. Name the three main Hindu gods.
3. What is an *avatar*?
4. When will Vishnu make his tenth and final visit to Earth?
5. Who are Vishnu's best-loved avatars?
6. Explain Hindu belief about Brahman. Your answer should cover the following points:
   - Brahman's relationship to the gods and the universe.
   - What Brahman contains.
   - Whether or not Brahman is a person.
7. What do Hindus believe about the differences between people, animals, fish and plants?
8. Explain the term *monism*.

The Varnas

Traditionally, Hinduism has taught that each person is born into a *varna* or a *caste* (i.e. a social group). The idea of caste has been traced back to about 1500 B.C. At that time a people called the Dravidians, who lived in northern India, were conquered by the Aryans. The Aryans set up a caste system to limit any contact between themselves and the defeated Dravidians.

This caste system divided people into four main groups.
- The *brahmins* were the highest caste and consisted of priests and teachers.
- Next came the *kshatriyas* who were the ruling nobles and warriors.
- Then the *vaishys* who were the merchants, craftsmen and farmers.
- Finally the *sudras* who were peasants and servants.

Lowest of all people were the *outcastes*, or those who existed outside the caste system. They were also called *untouchables*. The untouchables had to do what were considered to be the most menial (i.e. dirtiest) jobs, such as handling dead animals or cleaning the streets. Because they worked with dirt and blood, the untouchables were themselves declared *impure* (i.e. not clean). They were forbidden to ever touch caste members or to ever drink water from the same well.

The caste system included strict rules about every part of daily life. Each person's job was determined by his or her caste. Members of one caste could not marry, eat with, or work with members of another caste. To break these rules was punishable by *expulsion* from the caste system and a life as an untouchable.

The great Hindu holy man Mohandas Gandhi, known as *the Mahatma* (i.e. *Great Soul*), was especially concerned at the way in which the untouchables were treated. He tirelessly campaigned to improve their position. Instead of calling them *outcastes*, Gandhi called them *harijans*, which means *children of God*.

Since India became an independent state in 1947, its government has passed laws protecting the human rights of the untouchables. Some Hindus have begun relaxing the strict caste system, while others have abandoned it. However, recent reports indicate that the idea and practice of untouchability remains strong in many parts of India.

QUESTIONS

1. What is the meaning of the Hindu word *varna*?
2. Who set up the caste system? Why did they do so?
3. There are four main groups into which the caste system is divided. Name each of them and state who belongs to each of them.
4. Write a brief paragraph on those who exist *outside* the caste system – *the untouchables*.
5. How does the caste system affect the daily lives of Hindus?
6. Who was the *Mahatma*? What did he do for the untouchables?
7. Who are the *harijans*? What does this name mean?
8. What has the Indian government done for the untouchables since 1947?

Reincarnation

All the major religions teach that a human being consists of a body and a soul.
- The *body* is the visible, physical aspect of a person.
- The *soul* is the invisible, spiritual aspect of a person.

But they do *not* all agree on how they relate to each other or on what is meant by the soul.

For example:
- Judaism, Christianity and Islam teach that each person's soul is separate and unique to that person.
- In contrast, Hinduism teaches that a person's soul is *neither* separate *nor* unique.

Hindus refer to the soul as *atma*. They believe that each person's soul is merely a fragment of Brahman that has somehow fallen into our world of birth and death. An atma is *trapped* within a human body.

Hinduism teaches that the atma must go through a series of lives and endure a long cycle of birth, death and rebirth. This is called *samsara*.

In each cycle the atma takes on a new body and so is *reincarnated*.

Karma

Hindus believe in the Law of Karma which states:

> *From good must come good, from evil must come evil.*

The word *karma* can be translated as either *action* or *fate*. This is because Hindus believe that an atma's actions in one life decides its fate in the next.

It is for this reason that Hindus have been generally willing to accept the caste system. Many Hindus believe that an atma's caste in its present reincarnation is decided by its *actions* in its previous life. One who has led a good life may be reborn into a *higher* caste. One who has lived a bad life may be reborn into a *lower* caste, or even return in the body of an animal.

When a Hindu dies, his/her body, like a worn-out piece of clothing, is *cremated* (i.e. burned to ashes). The relatives may then scatter the ashes in a holy place, such as the river Ganges, as a sign that they hope that their loved one will be reborn into a higher caste or perhaps achieve *nirvana*.

Nirvana

Hindus believe that the soul or *atma* is trapped in a cycle of birth, death and rebirth. This is called *samsara*. The only way atma can escape this is to live a life of such goodness that it can achieve *spiritual perfection*. This is called *nirvana*.

When a very good and holy person dies, the atma finally achieves nirvana. It is released from this world. It returns to Brahman. It is then *re-absorbed* into Brahman like a drop of rain returning to the ocean.

The Hindu doctrine of Samsara. ➡

[Read this diagram from the bottom upwards.]

The Hindu View of Life

Once a soul has realised these things it does not need to be reborn into the physical world. The soul becomes united to Brahman and does not need a body.

Eventually the soul will be reborn as a person who will be able to live an unselfish life and who will understand that the things of the world don't count because they don't last.

Living a good life will mean that in the next life the soul will be reborn as a person who will be able to understand more about God.

Living a bad life will mean that in the next life the soul could be reborn as an animal, or it could mean suffering.

A soul is reborn many times before it becomes united with Brahman. Your action in one lifetime decides what your next life will be like.

Vegetarianism

Hindus are *vegetarians,* i.e. they do not eat any meat or fish. This is because of their belief in reincarnation.

Since all things are part of Brahman, Hindus believe that it would be wrong to kill a creature that is really no different from themselves. A dog or a salmon might be an atma at a different stage of its struggle to reach nirvana.

Hindus are expected to respect all animals, but cows are given special respect. A cow is said to care for human beings. Its milk gives nourishment and its dung is used as fuel for fire. The cow's gentle nature is seen as an example of how people should treat each other.

The Ten 'Rules'

Hindus have ten *rules* for living. Five are things one *should* do and five are things one should *not* do.

Don't ...	*Do ...*
destroy or injure anything	*keep yourself clean*
lie	*be contented*
steal	*be kind and patient*
be envious	*educate yourself*
be greedy	*try to give your mind to Brahman (or God)*

▲
Hindus are required by their religion to show respect for all living things.

◄
Almost every Hindu home has a household shrine with images of the gods and goddesses. *Puja* is the name given to Hindu worship. It involves offering flowers and/or food as an expression of devotion to the gods.

QUESTIONS

1. What do Jews, Christians and Muslims believe about a person's soul?
2. Do Hindus share this view of the soul?
3. What is the Hindu name for the soul?
4. What do Hindus believe about the soul?
5. Explain the meaning of *samsara*.
6. What is *reincarnation*?
7. State the *Law of Karma*.
8. Explain the meaning of the term *karma*.
9. What happens to the body of a Hindu once he/she dies?
10. What is *nirvana*?
11. What happens to the atma once it achieves nirvana?
12. Why are Hindus *vegetarians*?
13. Why are cows given special respect?
14. What are the ten *rules* for living?

▲

In the town of Puri, in India, a huge image of Krishna, called Jagannath, is displayed in procession each year. Jagannath travels in a massive chariot pulled by ropes. It is from this chariot that we derive the English word 'juggernaut', which means 'an unstoppable force'.

CHAPTER TWENTY

BUDDHISM

Introduction

Buddhism was founded by an Indian holy man named Siddhartha Gautama who was born in the foothills of the Himalayas around 565 B.C. He was raised a Hindu but later, in adult life, rejected it.

Since Buddhist scriptures were not organised or written down until almost six hundred years after Siddhartha's death, we cannot be certain about the exact historical details of his life. However, the account given here is that accepted by most Buddhists.

The Buddha

Siddhartha Gautama was an Indian prince, the son of an immensely rich nobleman. When he was born, a holy man informed Siddhartha's father that his son was destined for greatness. He would become either a powerful emperor or a great religious leader. Because he wanted Siddhartha to become a great ruler, his father isolated him from the outside world. Siddhartha grew up within the walls and gardens of his father's magnificent palace. He was shielded from the unpleasant aspects of life. His father feared that, if Siddhartha saw the world as it truly was, he might devote his life to religion rather than to politics.

As a young man Siddhartha married Princess Yosodhara. For ten years they lived together in

◄ A statue of the Buddha.

magnificent palaces surrounded by parks filled with all kinds of exotic birds and rare fish. They were followed by servants wherever they went. They wanted for nothing, completely protected from the harsh realities of the outside world. Eventually a son was born to them. Their lives seemed complete. It seemed as though Siddhartha's father had been successful.

When Siddhartha was about thirty-years-old, he made three trips outside his palace grounds. On these trips he encountered two men, one very old and one covered in sores. He also saw a corpse about to be cremated. For the first time Siddhartha learned about ageing, sickness and death. He was troubled that human beings had to suffer such tragedies.

On a fourth trip Siddhartha met a holy man. This man had nothing but a bowl for begging and a single yellow robe. Yet he looked very happy. Siddhartha realised that there was more to happiness than pleasure and possessions. He became deeply dissatisfied with his shallow, self-serving lifestyle. These four experiences which so disturbed Siddhartha are known as the *Four Sights*.

The Four Sights. ▲

Determined to find answers to the questions of suffering and the meaning of life, Siddhartha decided to leave his wife and newborn son. Slipping unnoticed out of the palace, he shaved his head, traded clothes with a beggar and left to seek truth, never to return. Buddhists still celebrate this event, which they call *the Blessed Night of the Great Renunciation*.

For several years afterwards, Siddhartha lived the life of a wandering monk. He sought guidance from the most respected Hindu *gurus* (i.e. teachers). He was advised to follow the *ascetic* path, i.e. to starve and pray for longer periods in order to gain wisdom. Siddhartha eventually realised that no deeper insight was coming and that he was only injuring himself. He carefully studied the *Vedas* (i.e. Hindu scriptures) but could not find the answers to his questions.

Finally, Siddhartha decided to find life's answers through his own thinking. One day, believed to be his thirty-fifth birthday, Siddhartha wandered into a village and sat down under a banyan tree. He decided to meditate (i.e. to quietly reflect) on all he had experienced and learned. By the following day he had at last *'pierced the bubble'* of the universe. He had at last gained *enlightenment*, i.e. a deep understanding of the meaning of life. The night during which he finally achieved this is called *the Sacred Night*. The banyan tree under which he sat is known as the *Bo Tree* (i.e. Tree of Wisdom).

▲
Shrine under the Bo Tree.

Siddhartha then travelled to Benares where he gave his first sermon. He taught that people could find freedom from suffering in *nirvana*, i.e. a state of complete happiness and peace. He said that suffering was caused by human desires. Therefore, by not desiring anything and by living correctly – avoiding extremes of self-denial and self-indulgence – a person would find peace.

Siddhartha soon attracted many followers and they showed their respect for him by calling him *Buddha*, which means *the Enlightened One*. His teachings gave rise to a new religion – Buddhism.

The Pali Canon

At first the stories and sayings of the Buddha were passed on *orally*, i.e. by word of mouth, as people related the stories and remembered many of the Buddha's sayings. As time passed, it became more important to write down his teachings so that no disagreements would arise between his followers. These were written down in Pali, an ancient North Indian language which was probably spoken by the Buddha.

The word *canon* means an agreed set of teachings.

The Pali Canon consists of 45 volumes. It is divided into three sections known as the *Tripitaka* (meaning *the Three Baskets*).

They are:

■ The *Vinaya* (i.e. *discipline basket*) which contains the rules for the Buddhist *Sangha* (i.e. community of monks and nuns).

Buddhist Pali scriptures. ▼

■ The *Sutta* (i.e. *instruction basket*) which consists of the Buddha's sermons.

■ The *Abhidhamma* (i.e. *great teaching basket*) which contains the Buddha's most profound and important teachings.

The *Pali Canon* was recorded by Buddhist monks and nuns living on Sri Lanka during the first century B.C. They wrote the text on manuscripts made from palm leaves.

QUESTIONS

1. When and where was Siddhartha Gautama born?
2. Why can we not be certain of the exact details of his life?
3. Why did Siddhartha's father isolate him from the harsh realities of the outside world?
4. Describe the kind of life Siddhartha led in his youth.
5. What *four* experiences led Siddhartha to change his way of life?
6. What happened on the *Blessed Night of the Great Renunciation*?
7. Explain the term *guru*.
8. What occurred on *the Sacred Night*?
9. What was the *Bo Tree*?
10. Where did Siddhartha give his first sermon?
11. What did he teach about:
    (a) *Nirvana* and
    (b) how people can find peace?
12. Why did Siddhartha Gautama's followers call him *Buddha*?
13. What is the *Pali Canon*? When was it written?
14. What is a *Sangha*?
15. What are the *Tripitaka* of the Pali Canon? What do they contain?

DEVOTION

Buddhists usually begin an act of devotion before a shrine by reciting the three refuges:

I take refuge in the Buddha
I take refuge in the Dharma
I take refuge in the Sangha

They may then bow three times before holy images or objects before making offerings or chanting.

BUDDHIST MONASTERIES

Monasteries house a community of monks or nuns who live there permanently, but they are also open to visitors, especially on festival days. The community formed by the first monks and nuns is known as the Sangha. The duty of the Sangha is to uphold and pass on the teachings of the Buddha.

A Buddhist temple usually contains shrine rooms, meditation and teaching halls as well as accommodation for the religious community.

THE BUDDHA

The Buddha drawn here is sitting in the lotus position. His outstretched arm is touching the earth which symbolises the Buddha's enlightenment.

DRUM AND BELL

The drum and bell in buildings (shown in cutaway) in the courtyard of the Buddhist temple are mainly used at festival times. Smaller bells in the shrine room are rung during daily devotions.

OFFERINGS

There will usually be various objects placed before the shrine:

Light from candles symbolises understanding
A shell symbolises sound
Food symbolises taste
Flowers symbolises sight
Incense and perfume symbolise smell
Water - there may be several pots of water symbolising touch, offering, healing, purification, satisfaction of thirst and of desires.

A Buddhist temple. ▲

Buddhist Teachings

Buddha accepted the Hindu doctrines of *karma* and *reincarnation*.

Karma

Buddha taught that everything that exists in all places and at all times is subject to the law of *karma* (i.e. the law of cause and effect). Buddha believed that all of a person's activities, whether they are his/her thoughts, words or deeds, are like seeds which will grow in this or some future life.

If a person does something wrong, it builds up *negative* karma. If a person does something good, it builds up *positive* karma.

The goal of life is to free oneself from negative karma and to create positive karma by living a good life.

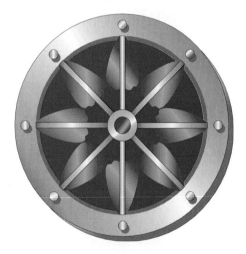

Reincarnation

Buddhists believe that human beings must endure a long cycle of birth, death and rebirth. People must spend several lives on Earth until they accumulate enough positive karma. Only then can they halt their long chain of rebirths and achieve the state of perfect peace called *nirvana*.

◄ The Buddhist Wheel of Life. The symbol of the ever turning eight-spoked Wheel of Law represents the important Middle Way taught by the Buddha and the ever turning and changing nature of life.

Achieving Nirvana

The Buddha taught his followers that, if they really wanted to achieve nirvana, then they would have to face up to the *Four Noble Truths*, as they have since been called by Buddhists. They are:

1. In this world, nothing lasts. Even the happiest moments pass away. There cannot be permanent happiness. The Buddhist word for the 'unsatisfactoriness' of life is *dukkha* (a word which means 'restlessness' or 'suffering').
2. *Dukkha* happens because people want more and more things and are never satisfied. They become greedy, envious and selfish.
3. But *dukkha* can cease if people overcome their selfishness, greed and hatred.
4. The way to do this is to follow the Eightfold Path.

The Eightfold Path

If a person is to follow the Eightfold Path, he/she must take eight steps i.e. try to do eight things in the correct or proper way. They are:

- **Understanding** *People should see clearly what they are doing with their lives.*
- **Thought** *They should not waste time daydreaming.*
- **Speech** *When they talk, they should say good things, not bad or cruel things.*
- **Deeds** *Good deeds are unselfish ones; people must not be selfish.*
- **Work** *People should try not to take jobs which will harm other living creatures.*
- **Effort** *People should try their best at all times.*
- **Mindfulness** *People should pay full attention to what they are doing.*
- **Concentration** *People should try to concentrate on what they have to do.*

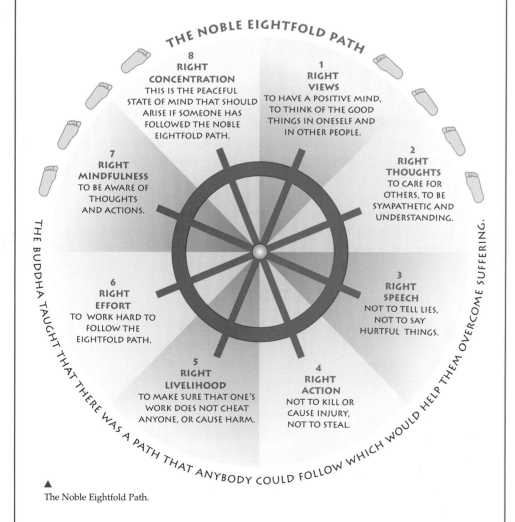

▲
The Noble Eightfold Path.

QUESTIONS

1. What did the Buddha teach about the law of *karma*?
2. What is the *goal of life* for Buddhists?
3. How can people halt the long chain of rebirths, according to Buddhism?
4. What did the Buddha teach about achieving nirvana?
5. What is the meaning of *dukkha*?
6. How can dukkha cease?
7. List the steps involved in following *the Eightfold Path*.

Do Buddhists Believe in God?

Remarkably, though Buddhism is considered a religion, the Buddha himself *ignored* the question of whether or not there is a God.

In the centuries that followed, the Buddha's followers debated the question and finally split into *two opposing groups* on this issue:

■ Those who were influenced by Hinduism and who, in time, came to consider the Buddha to have been a god.

They went on to develop elaborate forms of worship.

■ Those who believed that the Buddha's silence on the matter indicated that there was nothing worthwhile to be said.

They believed that the Buddha wanted his followers to *reject* the whole idea of worshipping an unseen, divine being. They also believed that the Buddha would have been *appalled* at the idea that his followers should worship him as a god.

The Spread of Buddhism

One of India's most famous kings, Asoka, who ruled during the third century B.C., was deeply influenced by the Buddha's teachings. He practised *tolerance* (i.e. respect) for all living things. Asoka sent Buddhist monks to spread the Buddha's teachings to other lands. Among them were his own son and daughter, who are said to have spread Buddhism to the island of Sri Lanka.

← Novice Buddhist monks.

Buddhism soon spread across Asia. It has helped to shape the lives and outlook of millions of people since, in countries such as Thailand, China, Tibet, Cambodia and Burma where, along with India, the greatest number of Buddhists now live. Recently, however, Buddhism has begun to attract followers in Europe and North America.

Zen Buddhism

A new form of Buddhism later arose called *Chen* in China and *Zen* in Japan. When most of us think deeply about a subject, we think in words. When we want to understand or explain something, we use words. But *Zen Buddhism* teaches people that words are only the surface of things, and that you must try to get beyond words in order to understand fully the meaning of life. As a result, followers of *Zen* may spend many years meditating on a single sentence that appears to make no sense, all the while trying to understand what lies beyond it.

A Buddhist monk at prayer.

QUESTIONS

1. What did the Buddha teach about God?
2. Why did Buddha's followers split into two groups?
3. (a) Who was *Asoka*?
   (b) Why is he an important figure in the history of Buddhism?
4. Name three modern countries where the majority of Buddhists live.
5. Where did *Zen Buddhism* originate?
6. What does *Zen Buddhism* teach about words?

CHAPTER TWENTY-ONE

ISLAM: PART ONE

The Meaning of Islam

Islam is an Arabic word which means *peace through submission, or giving oneself over, to the revealed will of God*. A follower of Islam is called a *Muslim*, i.e. one who submits.

Where it Began

The birthplace of Islam was the vast Arabian desert peninsula which lies between the north-west coast of Africa and central Asia. The people who lived there were known as *Arabs*. (The word 'Arab' means *nomad*.)

By the seventh century A.D. some of the Arab inhabitants of this harsh terrain had chosen to live in towns, but most were members of the *Bedouin*, a nomadic tribe who roamed the desert in search of grass and water for their herds.

A few of the region's inhabitants were Jews or Christians but the vast majority were *polytheists*.

At that time there was no strong, united kingdom in Arabia and the Bedouin tribes constantly fought among themselves over control of pastures and wells. All this was about to change.

The place where this change began was a town called *Mecca*, which had been built around an oasis in the mountainous area of

Bedouin Arabs. ▼

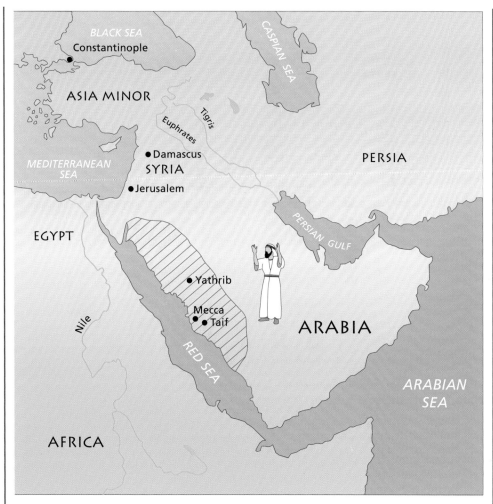

▲ The Middle East in the time of Muhammad.

western Arabia. It had developed into an important commercial centre because many traders stopped there for food and water on their way north to Constantinople and Damascus.

Arab *pilgrims* (i.e. those who went on a journey to pray at some holy place) also came to Mecca in large numbers to worship at Arabia's holiest shrine – *the Kaaba* (meaning: the *house of God*).

All early Arabs considered the Kaaba holy, no matter what gods they worshipped. It was a low, cube-shaped building, the size of a small house, built of grey stone. In the early seventh century it contained some three hundred and sixty *idols*, i.e. images or items which were worshipped by the polytheist pilgrims. The most important thing in the Kaaba, however, was a *Black Stone*, thought to be a meteorite, which was embedded in one wall. It was generally believed that this had fallen to earth from heaven.

▲ The Kaaba in the centre of Mecca.

According to Arab legend, the original Kaaba had stood in heaven. It was believed that the first humans had built the Kaaba in Mecca to look exactly like the one in heaven. Nearby, Ishmael, the legendary founder of the Arabs, was believed to have discovered a well, which became known as the *zemzen* (i.e. holy well). The town of Mecca grew up and prospered around both the Kaaba and the zemzen.

Pilgrims who came to worship at the Kaaba kissed the black stone and walked around the Kaaba seven times reciting prayers. Some left offerings before the idols.

By the late sixth century A.D., Christian and Jewish preachers had arrived in Mecca. They encouraged the people to turn away from worshipping idols and *astrology*, (i.e. studying the planets and stars in an attempt to foretell future events). These Christian and Jewish missionaries told the people of Mecca about a better way of life that would bring them peace and happiness. They taught that there was only *one* God. Most Meccans rejected them and continued as before. But among them was one who did listen – *Muhammad*.

N.B.
Muslim scriptures state that Abraham was a Muslim and that Arabs are descendants of Abraham's son Ishmael, while Jews are descendants of his other son Isaac.

QUESTIONS

1. Explain each of the following:
   (a) *Islam*
   (b) *Muslim*
   (c) *Arab*
2. Describe the *Kaaba* in Mecca *before* the coming of Islam.
3. What did Arab legends say about the Kaaba?
4. What was a *zemzen*?
5. Why were the idols in the Kaaba and the nearby zemzen important to the economy of Mecca?
6. What do Muslims believe about Abraham's sons, Ishmael and Isaac?
7. What is *astrology*?

The Call of Muhammad

Most of the details of Muhammad's life were not recorded until years after his death, but the basic story is well known. He was born in Mecca around the year A.D. 570. Orphaned at the age of six, Muhammad (meaning *highly praised*) was adopted by his uncle Abu Talib and grew up with his cousin Ali. As a boy, Muhammad worked on camel caravans, often travelling to the great trade centres of the Middle East. According to Muslim tradition, he was accompanying his uncle on a visit to Damascus, when they met a Christian monk who predicted that Muhammad would one day do great things in God's service.

As a young man Muhammad entered the employment of a rich widow named Khadijah. She found Muhammad to be a thoroughly good and very intelligent person. They married and were very happy together.

In time, Muhammad became a respected and successful businessman. However, he grew increasingly troubled by what he saw around him. Too many Meccans lived lives damaged by alcohol abuse and gambling. Corruption was widespread. Things had to change.

▲ A sixteenth-century drawing of Muhammad.

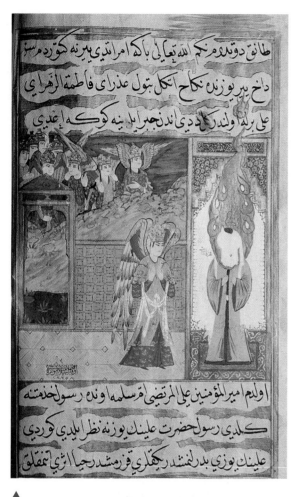

Drawing of the angel Gabriel appearing to Muhammad.

Muhammad began spending more and more time alone in a cave on Mount Hira, a few miles outside the city. There he prayed and fasted (i.e. went without food and water) for long periods.

Muhammad decided that the Arabs were being led into corruption and wickedness because they believed in false gods. He concluded that there was only one God – *Allah* (this is the Arabic word for *God*). This was the same God worshipped by the Jews and the Christians.

In A.D. 610, when he was about thirty-nine years of age, Muhammad is said to have received a *revelation* (i.e. a vision containing a message) from God. When he was alone in the cave on Mount Hira, the angel Gabriel appeared to him in a blaze of light and told Muhammad that he was to be the *prophet* of his people (i.e. the one who would tell them the will of God). This event is known as *the Night of Power and Excellence*.

Stunned by this extraordinary experience, Muhammad returned home and told his wife, Khadijah all that had happened. She listened carefully and, knowing Muhammad to be a good and honest man, she believed that God – *Allah* – had indeed spoken to Muhammad through the angel Gabriel. Khadijah and Muhammad's cousin Ali became his first disciples and the first converts to a new religion – *Islam*. In the difficult times ahead, Muhammad drew great strength from Khadijah's loving encouragement and support.

QUESTIONS

1. What does the name *Muhammad* mean?
2. Write a brief note on Muhammad's early life.
3. Who was Khadijah?
4. How did Muhammad react to the corruption and injustice he witnessed in Mecca?
5. Where did he go to pray and to discover what God wanted of him?

QUESTIONS CONTD

6. What conclusions did Muhammad reach about (a) the sources of the corruption and wickedness of Mecca and (b) God?
7. Describe Muhammad's extraordinary experience, which Muslims refer to as *the Night of Power and Excellence*. When and where did it happen?
8. Muhammad was told that he had been chosen to be the *prophet* of Allah. What does this mean?
9. Who were Muhammad's first disciples and converts to Islam?

The Message

After a while, Muhammad received another revelation in which he was ordered to *rise and warn* the people. So, in A.D. 613, Muhammad began preaching to the people of Mecca. He told them that:

- There is only one God – *Allah* – who is all-powerful. Therefore, the people should abandon polytheism and worship *only* Allah.
- All believers are *equal* before Allah. Anyone, of whatever race or colour, can become a Muslim.
- Nothing happens except by the will of Allah. People must trust in Allah's wisdom and goodness without question.
- The rich must share with the poor because Allah measures a person's worth by his/her good deeds and devotion to Him.
- People should live their lives in preparation for *the Day of Judgment* (i.e. the last day) when Allah will hold all accountable for their actions; rewarding the good and punishing the wicked in the next world.

A Hostile Reaction

At first the wealthy businessmen and religious leaders of Mecca didn't take Muhammad seriously. But very soon they began to change their attitude towards him. Muhammad demanded that all idols be removed from the Kaaba. This was a direct threat to the business activities of those Meccans who had been making healthy profits from the many pilgrims who came to worship those idols.

Opponents of Muhammad realised that he would not stop until he had destroyed every idol and had introduced fairness and justice to the government of their city. They accused Muhammad of trying to wreck the local economy. Mecca's leaders began persecuting Muhammad and his followers. Threats on his life grew more and more frequent. But Muhammad refused to be intimidated.

The Departure to Medina

In A.D. 620 Muhammad preached to a group of pilgrims from the city of Yathrib, about two hundred and seventy miles north of Mecca. They invited Muhammad to come to Yathrib and be their leader.

During the summer of A.D. 622, Muhammad and several hundred of his followers left Mecca to make a fresh start in Yathrib. This departure from Mecca is called *the Hegira* (i.e. the departure or emigration). Just as Christians mark the beginning of the Christian era by Jesus' birth, Muslims begin their calendar with Muhammad's move from Mecca. The year A.D. 622 is the *first* year of the Muslim calendar. The city of Yathrib was later renamed *Medina*, (i.e. the city of the prophet) in Muhammad's honour.

In Medina, Muhammad proved a great political leader as well as a religious one. He soon gained a huge following there and took control of its government. Muhammad made sure that widows and orphans were cared for and that the poor were given food and shelter. His fair and honest rule united the people of Medina and made them proud of their city. Muhammad responded to any praise by saying that without the guidance of Allah he could not have achieved anything. People now began to refer to Muhammad as the *Rasul*, or Messenger, of Allah.

QUESTIONS

1. When did Muhammad begin publicly preaching in Mecca?
2. What did he teach about
   - *Allah*
   - *equality*
   - *sharing*
   - *the Day of Judgment*?
3. Why did the wealthy businessmen begin to consider Muhammad a threat?
4. What did they accuse Muhammad of trying to do?
5. How did Muhammad's powerful enemies try to stop him?
6. (a) What is the *Hegira*?
   (b) Why is this an important date on the Muslim calendar?
7. Why was Yathrib later renamed *Medina*?
8. By what title did Muhammad's followers begin to refer to him?

The Return To Mecca

Muhammad was determined to return to Mecca and to convert its people to Islam. He decided to wage a *jihad* (i.e. a holy war) against the opponents of Islam. After three major battles, Muhammad led ten thousand of his followers in victory into Mecca in A.D. 630.

Muhammad went directly to the Kaaba and had all the idols removed and destroyed. However, he preserved the Kaaba itself because he believed that Abraham had originally built it for the worship of Allah, but that others had later abused this holy place. Muhammad ordered that from this time on the Kaaba would stand empty except for the *Black Stone*, which he believed had been given to Abraham by the angel Gabriel. Before long, Mecca became the centre of Islam.

▲ Muhammad and his men poised to attach Mecca.

The Death of Muhammad

In A.D. 631 delegates representing Arabs from all over Arabia came to declare their faith in Allah and to offer their allegiance to Muhammad. He had united the Arabs into a single state with a powerful army. However, in A.D. 632, Muhammad fell ill and died at Medina. He was succeeded by a series of *caliphs*, i.e. successors. They continued his campaign to win the world for Islam and, within a century of Muhammad's death, Islam had taken root as far west as Spain and as far east as India.

▲ Muhammad's ascension into heaven.

The expansion of Islam. ▼

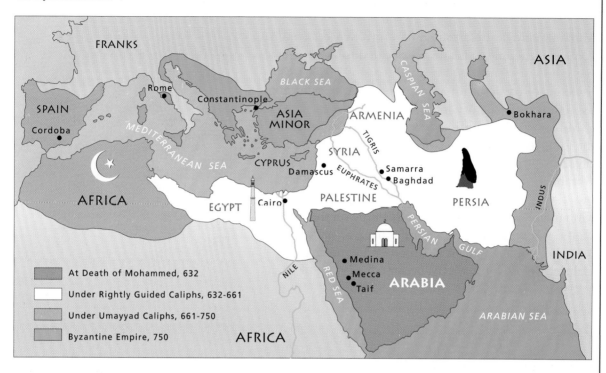

QUESTIONS

1. Explain the Arabic word *jihad*.
2. Why did Muhammad order the Kaaba to be preserved once the idols were removed?
3. Why was the *Black Stone* left in the Kaaba?
4. What did Muhammad achieve in A.D. 631?
5. Who were the *caliphs*?

CHAPTER TWENTY-TWO

ISLAM: PART TWO

Introduction

Muslims believe that *Allah is the Lord of all*. Since the death of Muhammad, Muslims have spread their message from Arabia to every continent, especially Africa and Asia. Today, approximately one-fifth of the world's population is *Muslim*.

Islam teaches that all people come from God and that they will return to God upon their deaths. Then, they will be rewarded or punished in accordance with how they have fulfilled their duty to God and to their fellow human beings.

Muslims believe that the clearest guidance as to how people should live is to be found in the *Qur'an*.

The Qur'an

The heart of Islam is the holy book known as the *Qur'an*, whose name means *that which is to be read*. Originally written in Arabic, the *Qur'an* is about four-fifths the size of the *New Testament* and is divided into 114 *surahs* (i.e. chapters). The whole text is prefaced by the opening surah which became the model for Islamic prayer:

> *Praise be to God, Lord of the world;*
> *The compassionate, the merciful*
> *King on the day of reckoning:*
> *Thee only do we worship, and*
> *to Thee do we cry for help.*
> *Guide Thou us on the straight*
> *path, the path of those to whom*
> *Thou has been gracious,*
> *With whom Thou are not angry,*
> *and who do not stray.*

▲
The star and crescent moon are important symbols in Islam. One reason is that in hot countries people travel in the cool of the night and the stars and moon guide them. These heavenly bodies guide and give light in the same way that Islam guides the faithful.

← Extract from the Qur'an.

Islam

'If all the humans and spirits joined together they could not write a book like the Qur'an.'

These words from the Qur'an form the centre of this pattern. Muslims believe that the Qur'an contains the Word of God, revealed to the Prophet Muhammad.

Muhammad claimed that the *Qur'an* was dictated to him word for word by God's messenger – the angel Gabriel. The *Qur'an* is revered as a miracle of God by Muslims, because Muhammad is said to have been *illiterate*, i.e. unable to read and write.

The *Qur'an* identifies the basic beliefs of Islam and gives strict guidelines for Muslim life. For example, according to the *Qur'an*, Muslims should not eat pork, nor drink alcoholic beverages nor gamble. It also gives advice on marriage, divorce, inheritance of property and business dealings. Further, it lays down strict punishment for theft, including cutting off a thief's right hand if he persists in wrongdoing.

Today the *Qur'an* rivals the *Bible* as the world's most widely read book.

The Five Articles of Faith

Every Muslim accepts the following *five* doctrines:
1. Allah is the one true God.
2. Angels are the instruments or messengers of Allah.
3. The *Qur'an* is the final and most complete revelation of Allah.
4. There have been twenty-eight prophets of Allah, of whom Muhammad was the last.
5. There will be a final day of judgment, when Allah will reward the good and punish the wicked.

Belief must lead to *action*. Muslims are expected to express and uphold their beliefs in their daily lives. They do so by practising *the five pillars of faith*.

QUESTIONS

1. What does the title *Qur'an* mean?
2. In what language was the *Qur'an* originally written?
3. How is the *Qur'an* organised?
4. Why is the *Qur'an* considered a miracle by Muslims?
5. State the five articles of Muslim faith.

The Five Pillars

The *Qur'an* describes *the five pillars of faith* or five duties which arise out of Muslim belief and which all Muslims are obliged to fulfil.

THE FIRST PILLAR: **SHAHADAH**

This is the acceptance of the idea that there is one and only one God - *Allah*. All Muslims are expected to say the following prayer:

> *There is no God but Allah, and Muhammad is his prophet.*

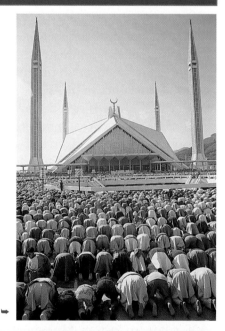

Muslims at prayer. ➡

THE SECOND PILLAR: **SALAT**

This involves commitment to daily prayer. Muslims must turn towards Mecca and pray five times each day – at dawn, midday, afternoon, evening and nightfall – wherever they are.

On Fridays, Muslims are expected to attend a mosque at midday for communal worship. There is no priesthood in Islam. Instead, *imams* lead the people in prayer and *mullahs* explain Islamic beliefs to the people.

THE THIRD PILLAR: ZAKAT

This concerns the giving of *alms* (i.e. charity). There are *two* kinds of alms. One is the money Muslims donate freely on their own initiative. The other is the part of a Muslim's income (set at one-fortieth) that is collected by the state. This is called *poor-due*. It is used to fund education and social services for the poor and sick.

THE FOURTH PILLAR: SAUM

This involves *fasting*, i.e. abstaining from food and drinking only water. The *Qur'an* states that the following do *not* have to fast: children, pregnant women, people who are ill or those making a long journey. Everyone else must fast each day during the daylight hours of the month of *Ramadan*, the ninth month of the Muslim year.

THE FIFTH PILLAR: HAJJ

This concerns the commitment every Muslim must make to go on pilgrimage to Mecca at least once in his/her lifetime. This journey is called the *hajj*. It should take place two months after *Ramadan*. It involves three days of ceremony and prayer during which Muslims from all over the world come together.

The Kaaba in Mecca. ▼

God in the Qur'an

Muslims believe that God – *Allah* – is an awesome, but distant being who is in control of human history. Muhammad believed that human beings were unworthy of God's attention. Out of his profound love and respect for Allah, Muhammad taught his followers that Allah is so great and so good that Allah is utterly different from human beings.

This emphasis on the holiness and separateness of Allah can be seen in the

Qur'an's instruction forbidding any artist from ever attempting to either draw or paint an image of Allah. Indeed, one of the greatest sins in Islam is *shirk* (i.e. blasphemy). This sin can be committed by trying to associate anything such as an image or a person with Allah. Muslims believe that Allah is good beyond compare.

This is why mosques and other Muslim buildings are usually decorated with *geometric patterns* (i.e. ones made up of lines and angles). Muslims believe that the beauty of these patterns reflects the beauty and unity of God's creation.

Though richly decorated, mosques bear no images of Allah. ➡

QUESTIONS

1. Match the names in column *B* with the appropriate pillar of Islam in column *A*.

A	B
First pillar	Saum
Second pillar	Hajj
Third pillar	Shahadah
Fourth pillar	Salat
Fifth pillar	Zakat

2. Briefly explain each of the five pillars.
3. What are (a) an *imam* and (b) a *mullah*?
4. What did Muhammad teach his followers about Allah?
5. What does the *Qur'an* forbid artists from doing?
6. (a) What is *shirk*?
   (b) How do Muslims believe this can be committed?
7. Why are mosques and other Muslim buildings decorated with geometric patterns?

Worship

The word *mosque* means *a place of prostration*. The mosque is usually a rectangular building to which Muslims come to pray. It is here also that Muslim children are taught the *Qur'an*. In Muslim countries one may hear the *muezzin* (i.e. the prayer caller) summoning the faithful to prayer from the balcony of the *minaret*, i.e. a tall slender tower attached to the mosque. Muslim women usually remain at home to pray, whereas Muslim men gather at the mosque on Fridays at midday. Attendance on Friday, the Lord's day, is compulsory.

Diagram of a mosque. ➡

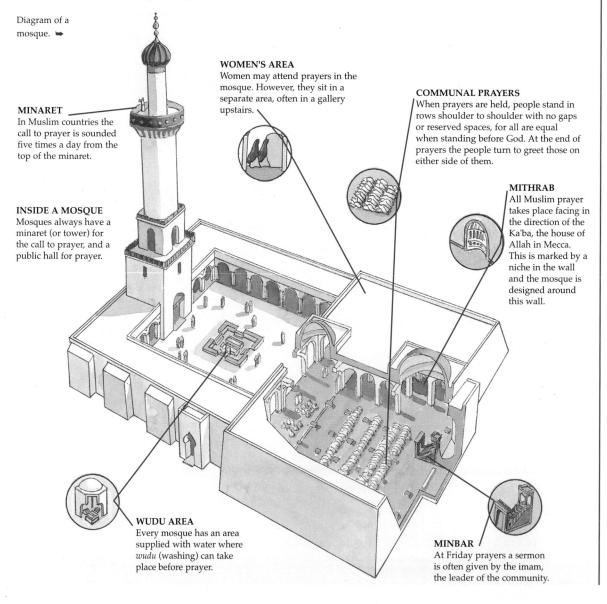

WOMEN'S AREA
Women may attend prayers in the mosque. However, they sit in a separate area, often in a gallery upstairs.

COMMUNAL PRAYERS
When prayers are held, people stand in rows shoulder to shoulder with no gaps or reserved spaces, for all are equal when standing before God. At the end of prayers the people turn to greet those on either side of them.

MINARET
In Muslim countries the call to prayer is sounded five times a day from the top of the minaret.

INSIDE A MOSQUE
Mosques always have a minaret (or tower) for the call to prayer, and a public hall for prayer.

MITHRAB
All Muslim prayer takes place facing in the direction of the Ka'ba, the house of Allah in Mecca. This is marked by a niche in the wall and the mosque is designed around this wall.

WUDU AREA
Every mosque has an area supplied with water where *wudu* (washing) can take place before prayer.

MINBAR
At Friday prayers a sermon is often given by the imam, the leader of the community.

When Muslims arrive at the mosque they remove their shoes at the entrance and cover their heads with a skullcap. In every mosque there is a fountain for ritual purification. Muslims wash themselves, a custom which may have been influenced by Christian baptism. Then, since there are no seats in a mosque, they unroll their prayer mats. Kneeling on their mats, they face in the direction of Mecca, as indicated by a *mithrab*, i.e. a recess in one wall of the mosque. There are no images or pictures in the mosque as the *Qur'an* forbids any pictorial representation of Allah.

When they have listened to the sermon, the faithful pray according to a *set* ritual. All Muslims follow the same prayer format as a reminder that they form one worldwide community of faith in Allah. A different position is taken as each part of the prayer is said:

These are a few of the words and positions of prayer, which is always said in Arabic.

Through wudu, the ritual washing, Muslims prepare for prayer in mind, body and spirit.

God is most great.

O God, glory and praise are for You, and blessed is Your name, and exalted is Your majesty; there is no god but You.

God is most great.

Glory to my Lord, the Highest.

God is most Great.

▲ A Muslim at prayer.

Each *gesture* has a specific meaning. For example:

- When a Muslim *stands*, it is to show his/her willingness to *listen* to Allah.
- When a Muslim *bows*, it is to show *respect* for Allah.
- When a Muslim *prostrates* him/herself it is to show *obedience* to the will of Allah.

QUESTIONS

1. Explain the meaning of the word *mosque*.
2. What is the role of the *muezzin*?
3. Who attends the mosque on Fridays?
4. How does a Muslim prepare for prayer when he arrives at a mosque?
5. What is a *mithrab*? What is its purpose?
6. Why are there no pictures or images in a mosque?
7. Why do Muslims all follow the same prayer format?
8. Explain the meaning of the following *gestures* made by Muslims when at prayer:
   - standing upright,
   - bowing,
     and
   - lying prostrate on the ground.

Naming and Initiation

The birth of a child is regarded as *barakah*, i.e. a blessing from Allah. A child cannot become a Muslim until he/she is old enough to *choose* to become one, at about the age of ten. However parents are expected to raise their children in the ways of Islam. Indeed, shortly after the child is born, the father will hold the infant close and whisper the *shahadah* into each ear:

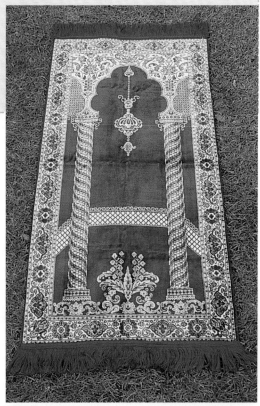

▲ A Muslim prayer mat.

There is no God but Allah and Muhammad is his Prophet.

This is done so that the very first words the child hears are about Allah and his prophet.

On the seventh day after the child's birth, the ritual of *Aqiqa*, i.e. the naming ceremony, is held. The child's head is shaved and money is given to charity, by tradition gold or silver of the same weight as the child's hair but in practice often more. Then sheep are sacrificed (two for a boy and one for a girl). The meat is then sweetened and divided out: one-third to relatives and two-thirds to the poor.

The child is given either one of Muhammad's names or one of his family names or one of Allah's ninety-nine names, with the Arabic word *Abd* (meaning: *servant*) added. Sometimes the parents ask the imam to choose a name for the baby.

Boys are often *circumcised* at *Aqiqa* (i.e. the top part of the loose foreskin over the penis is cut off). However, this can be done at any time up to the age of ten.

Education

Children are considered to be able to distinguish right from wrong by the age of seven and so religious education starts then. Children usually attend *Qur'an* classes in the local mosque. At this point children learn to read and write Arabic, if the language is not spoken by the family in the home.

◄ A Muslim boy reading the Qur'an.

QUESTIONS

1. How do Muslims look upon the birth of a child?
2. When does a child become a Muslim?
3. What is a Muslim father expected to do shortly after the child is born?
4. What is *Aqiqa*?
5. Why is the baby's head shaved?
6. Explain the Arabic word *Abd*.
7. What is *circumcision*?
8. At what age do Muslim children begin their religious education?

CHAPTER TWENTY-THREE

ISLAM: PART THREE

The Hajj

The hajj or pilgrimage to the city of Mecca, Islam's holiest place, is one of the religious duties of every Muslim. It is also something to which every devout Muslim eagerly looks forward. To visit the *Kaaba* in the holy city of Islam is, for the faithful, the fulfilment of a life's ambition. It must only be undertaken when a Muslim has settled all his outstanding debts and attended to all his family commitments.

The hajj takes place between the seventh and the thirteenth of *Dhu al-hijja*, the final month in the Muslim year.

When they arrive at the city of Mecca, all male pilgrims must put on a white seamless garment called the *ihram* and walk barefoot. This is intended to show the equality of all men before Allah. Women, however, are not expected to wear any special garment.

Everyone is expected to follow set rituals and guides ensure that this is done:

1. First, all pilgrims pass round the Kaaba seven times – three times quickly and four times slowly – in an anti-clockwise direction, kissing or touching the black stone as they pass.

2. They then pass between the hills Safa and Marwa seven times, remembering Ishmael's mother, Hagar, who ran between the hills looking for water. Ishmael found a spring, which is now called the Zemzem.

3. Next they proceed to Mount Arafat, thirteen miles away where they offer prayers.

4. At Mina, a small village, stones are thrown at a pillar. Pilgrims remember how Satan tried to tempt Ishmael to turn against his father when he was about to sacrifice him and how he threw stones at Satan to frighten him away. A sacrifice of a sheep is made here, just as Abraham offered a sheep, instead of Ishmael, to God.*

5. On returning to Mecca, pilgrims pass around the Kaaba again.

The grand finale of the hajj is the feast of *Eid-ul-Adha*, which we shall examine later.

---

* Jews believe that it was Abraham's other son Isaac, rather than Ishmael.

The hajj has great importance for Muslims. They believe that Allah forgives all the sins of those who make the journey in a spirit of *reverence* (i.e. deep respect). Anyone who dies on the journey to or from Mecca is considered a *martyr* (i.e. someone who has died for his/her beliefs), and is said to be taken directly to heaven by Allah.

1
All the pilgrims put on the same clothes – two plain white sheets.

2
The pilgrims enter Haraam, the sacred area around Mecca where only Muslims can go.

3
They go into the Great Mosque, where they walk seven times around the Kaaba.

4
The pilgrims run seven times between Mecca and Marwa. This reminds them of Hagar searching for water for her son. Then they drink at the Zemzem well.

The Hajj route. ▲

5
The pilgrims walk five miles to Mina to spend the night praying and meditating.

6
Then they go to the plain of Arafat where they pray and meditate.

7
On the way back, they spend the night at Muzdaliffah. Then they go back to Mina, where they throw stones at pillars (which are symbols of the devil), before returning to Mecca.

QUESTIONS

1. What is Islam's holiest place?
2. When does the hajj take place?
3. (a) What is the *ihram*?
   (b) Who wears it?
   (c) Why do they wear it?
4. Write a brief account outlining the set rituals in which Muslims participate during the hajj.
5. Why is the hajj of great importance for Muslims?

Festivals

Islam has its own calendar. It has twelve months but each month is only twenty-nine or thirty days long because it follows the lunar cycle, i.e. the time between one new moon and the next. As a result, the Muslim year is eleven days shorter than that of Jews and Christians. Muslims date their era from the year A.D. 622 when the prophet Muhammad emigrated from Mecca.

Eid or *id* is the Muslim word for a festival. This is a large scale communal celebration which seeks to engender a spirit of friendship and goodwill. Visitors and strangers are welcomed and special provisions are made for the poor.

The following are the key festivals of Islam:

Hijrah

This celebration marks the beginning of the Muslim year and it is a time to recall the journey made by the prophet Muhammad from Mecca to Medina in A.D. 622. Muslims celebrate the establishment of their religious community and gifts are often exchanged.

Eid-ul-Fitr

This festival comes at the end of the month of Ramadan, the ninth month of the Muslim calendar.

Ramadan is important because Muslims believe that it was during this month that Allah revealed himself to Muhammad through the angel Gabriel. Muslims fast (i.e. abstain from food, drink and sexual intercourse) during the daylight hours throughout this month. *Eid-ul-Fitr* marks the end of Ramadan.

Eid-ul-Fitr is also called *the small festival*. It lasts for three days and is celebrated with special prayers. It is a time for visiting friends and holding a large family meal. New clothes are often bought and children also receive presents of money and sweets. The poor are not forgotten. It is customary to send them food.

Eid-ul-Fitr is a celebration not only of the end of a long period of fasting, but of a challenge successfully faced.

Eid-ul-Adha

This is also known as the *great feast* or *the festival of sacrifice*. It lasts for four days and is held within the final month of the Muslim year. In this festival:

■ Muslims celebrate the completion of the annual pilgrimage to Mecca. They rejoice in their shared identity and reflect on their responsibilities as a community of worshippers established by the prophet Muhammad.

■ Muslims remember the willingness of Abraham to sacrifice his son Ishmael as an act of complete submission to Allah and how Allah intervened to prevent the boy's death.

As a *symbol* of their own willingness to submit completely to Allah, Muslims traditionally sacrifice a sheep and then enjoy a family meal. There may be an exchange of gifts and cards.

This festival is also a time to give help to those less fortunate. Part of the meat in the celebration meal is traditionally given to poorer families.

QUESTIONS

1. From what year do Muslims date their era?
2. What is this year according to the Muslim method of dating?
3. Match the correct explanation in column *B* with the festival name in column *A*.

A FESTIVAL	B EXPLANATION
Hijrah	Marks the end of Ramadan.
Eid-ul-Fitr	Held in the final month of the Muslim year and celebrates the completion of the annual pilgrimage to Mecca.
Eid-ul-Adha	Marks the beginning of the Muslim year.

4. Which festival recalls the journey made by the prophet Muhammad from Mecca to Medina?
5. Why is Ramadan important for Muslims?
6. Why is the Eid-ul-Adha also known as *the festival of sacrifice*?
7. In what ways are the poor and less fortunate remembered in Muslim festivals?

Divisions

All devout Muslims revere the Qur'an and strive to carry out the five pillars. When Muhammad died, however, there were disputes about who should succeed him and so *divisions* arose among Muslims. Loretta Pastva offers the following account of the deep split within Islam between the majority *Sunni* Muslims and the minority *Shia* Muslims.

The Shia Muslims broke with the Sunni Muslims over the issue of the leadership of Islam. The **Sunnis** believe that the caliph, the spiritual and secular successor to Muhammad, must be a member of Muhammad's tribe, the Koreish. The Sunnis elect the caliph.

On the other hand, the **Shias** (sometimes called Shiites) believe that Muhammad intended to establish a hereditary line of religious leaders, called **Imams**, to teach and guide the faithful. **Ali**, the husband of Fatimah, is identified as the first Imam. (This word Imam is often written with a capital I to distinguish it from the imams who are the local religious leaders of the Sunnis.) Shias hold that the Imam is a God-given post that is open only to descendants of Muhammad through Ali.

Because the current version of the Qur'an does not mention the name of Ali, the Shias reason that the Qur'an must have been tampered with by Ali's enemies. Therefore, the Shias are suspicious of traditional readings and interpretations of the Qur'an, searching instead for hidden meanings in its words. The world view of the Shias has been heavily coloured by their deep distrust of the present world order. Thus, they look to the future when a promised messiah will bring justice to the oppressed.

The majority of Muslims are Sunnis. But the Shias are the dominant sect in Iran, Pakistan, and Lebanon. Conflicts between Sunnis and Shias have frequently occurred. On several occasions Shia Muslims have attempted to wrest the control of the sacred Kaaba in Mecca from the Sunnis.

Adapted from – *Great Religions of the World.*
St Mary's Press.

QUESTIONS

1. Identify the two main groups within Islam. State which is the majority group and which is the minority one.
2. On what issue did these two groups split apart?
3. Explain the beliefs about the leadership of Islam among
   (a) the *Sunnis* and
   (b) the *Shias*.
4. (a) Who do Shias recognise as the *Imam*?
   (b) What to they believe about the *Imam*?
5. Why do Shias believe that someone has tampered with the current version of the *Qur'an*?
6. Describe the Shia attitude to interpreting the *Qur'an*.
7. (a) How do Shias look upon the present world order?
   (b) What do they hope for in the future?

Relations With Other Religions

Muslims believe that Islam did not begin with the prophet Muhammad. The message of Allah was revealed to a number of holy men long before Muhammad was born. Muslims believe that Adam, Abraham, Moses and Jesus were also Allah's prophets. However, Muhammad stands apart from these earlier prophets. They believe that he is the *last*, the *greatest* and the *most decisive* prophet of Allah.

While Muslims recognise that the words of Allah may be found in the *Torah*, the *Psalms* and the *Gospels*, they believe that they are mixed up with too many human additions. Islam teaches that the *pure* word of God is *only* to be found in the *Qur'an*. As a result they believe that Islam is the only religion with the *complete* truth.

For this reason, devout Muslims believe that it is their solemn duty to encourage others to follow the way of *Islam*, (i.e. of submission to the will of Allah). However, the *Qur'an* expressly *forbids* forcing people to believe what they do not want to believe. This is because Allah has given all people the gifts of reason and free choice. Such gifts are to be respected. As surah 2, verse 257 states:

> *Let there be no compulsion in religion.*

Other religions are to be respected and missionary work should be carried out in such a way as not to give offence.

QUESTIONS

1. Name four holy men who lived before Muhammad whom Muslims accept as prophets of Allah.
2. Why do Muslims believe that Muhammad stands apart from the earlier prophets of Allah?
3. (a) What do Muslims believe about the *Torah*, the *Psalms* and the *Gospels*?
   (b) What do they believe about the *Qur'an*?
   (c) How does this affect the way they view their own religion?
4. Explain the teaching of the *Qur'an* about respecting the religious beliefs of other non-Muslim peoples.

We shall return to consider other aspects of Muslim life in *Book Three*.

SIKHISM

Sikhism was founded by a holy man named *Nanak* in the Punjab in Northern India in the fifteenth century. Although the region at that time was ruled over by the Muslim Mughal empire, the majority of its people were Hindus. This led to great tension between Hindu and Muslim populations.

Nanak was convinced that all people were brothers and sisters in God's eyes. He believed that there was good in *both* Hinduism and Islam. He drew insights from both Hinduism and Islam to establish the youngest of the world's major religions – Sikhism. He spent his life travelling and teaching and became knows as *Guru Nanak* ('Guru' means *teacher*).

Sikhs are monotheists. They refer to God as *Waheguru*, meaning '*Great Teacher*'. A Sikh place of worship is known as a *gurdwara*, the most famous of which is the *Harimandir* (i.e. House of God) in Amritsar, more widely known as *the Golden Temple*.

The holy book of Sikhism is called the *Guru Granth Sahib*. It is given a place of special honour in a Sikh temple.

Christianity and Other Religions

All the Christian traditions believe in religious freedom. They all teach that human beings are *invited* and *not* forced to worship God. People have a right to choose whether or not they wish to belong to a particular religion.

Christianity Judaism Islam

Hinduism Buddhism

At the Second Vatican Council (1962-1965), the leaders of the Catholic Church stated that

> *The Church condemns, as foreign to the mind of Christ, any discrimination against people or any harassment of them on the basis of their race, colour, condition in life or religion.*

However, the Catholic Church teaches that people have a duty to inform themselves about the teachings of any particular religion and reflect seriously on them before deciding to accept or reject membership.

The Catholic Church calls on its members to build *bonds of friendship* with non-Christians of good character and states that Christians should *reject nothing that is true and holy in other religions.*

This, however, raises an important question: Why choose to be a Christian rather than a Jew, Muslim, Hindu or Buddhist?

Christians answer this question by saying that Jesus Christ revealed God's love for human beings in a way and in a depth which is utterly *unique*. In Jesus, God became a human being and lived on Earth. He died for people's sins and rose from the dead. God is not a remote being, but very close to people. This is why Jesus is called *Emmanuel*, meaning: *God-with-us.* Christians claim that there is nothing like this in any other religion.

Christians respectfully accept that other religions do contain important insights into the mystery of God and the great questions of human life. However, they believe that *only Christianity contains the whole truth about God and the meaning of life.*

An *icon* of Jesus. The word *icon* comes from the Greek word meaning *image*. Icons are usually richly decorated paintings of Jesus, Mary, a saint or an angel. All the details in an icon are designed to convey important religious teachings. ➥

QUESTIONS

1. What is meant by *religious freedom*?
2. Explain the teaching of the Catholic Church on the issue of religious freedom.
3. Why are Christians called to build *bonds of friendship with non-Christians of good character*?
4. *Christians believe that Jesus Christ revealed the love of God for human beings in a way and in a depth which is utterly unique.*
   What reasons do Christians put forward to support this belief?

JOURNAL WORK

Read the following statement:

The difference between Christianity and the other religions is not basically the difference between truth and error, but between total and partial understanding.

Bishop Stephen Neill (Church of England) quoted in *The Lion Handbook of Christian Belief.*

In your own words, explain what this statement means.

Part Six

Challenges to Religion

CHAPTER TWENTY-FOUR

RELIGION AND SCIENCE: CONFLICT

Introduction

Religion has been practised by human beings for more than *sixty five thousand years*. Science, in contrast, is a relative newcomer. It has only made a real impact on how people think in the last *five hundred years*.

For many centuries, the important position religion held in society was *unchallenged*. Religion seemed to provide people with the answers to so many of the questions that concerned them.

Consider, for example, the farmer who wants a good harvest. This depends on the land he works being *fertile*, i.e. able to produce crops.

In ancient times, Egyptian farmers prayed to the god *Osiris* to grant them a successful harvest. They believed that Osiris was responsible for the soil being fertile.

Today, Egyptian farmers would most likely give the credit for a good harvest to *fertilisers*. They see things *very differently* from their ancestors. This change is due to the impact of *science* on the way human beings understand the world in which they live.

▲
Egyptian god Osiris accepts offerings.

What is Science?

The word *science* comes from the Latin word *scientia* meaning *knowledge*.

Generally speaking, *science* refers to any area of study where knowledge is gained:

1. by careful *observation* of how things work or how events happen in the world
2. by conducting *experiments* to test our ideas about these things or events
3. by only accepting or rejecting any explanation of such things or events if one has good *reasons* for doing so.

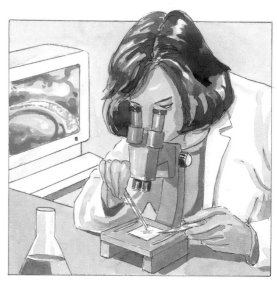

Closely linked to science is *technology*. We may define technology as

the practical application of scientific discoveries to everyday life.

Science has been very successful in answering a huge range of questions about how the world works. Technology has changed the whole way in which so many people live. This has led some people to wonder if religion has anything important to offer today.

Some people think that science has shown religion to be *worthless*. For example, the scientist Richard Dawkins has commented that:

Science has nothing to learn from religion and neither does anyone else.

Some people claim that, one day, science will *take over* from religion altogether. They believe that science can provide the answers to *all* the important questions facing humanity.

Others, among them many scientists, *disagree* with this. They say that those who claim that science will eventually replace religion are

Scientific and technological achievement.
▼

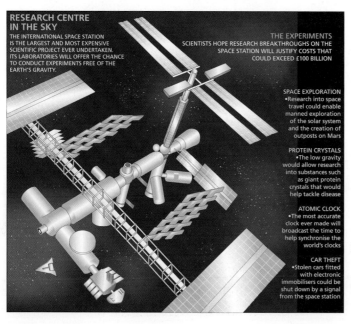

RESEARCH CENTRE IN THE SKY
THE INTERNATIONAL SPACE STATION IS THE LARGEST AND MOST EXPENSIVE SCIENTIFIC PROJECT EVER UNDERTAKEN. ITS LABORATORIES WILL OFFER THE CHANCE TO CONDUCT EXPERIMENTS FREE OF THE EARTH'S GRAVITY.

THE EXPERIMENTS
SCIENTISTS HOPE RESEARCH BREAKTHROUGHS ON THE SPACE STATION WILL JUSTIFY COSTS THAT COULD EXCEED £100 BILLION

SPACE EXPLORATION
•Research into space travel could enable manned exploration of the solar system and the creation of outposts on Mars

PROTEIN CRYSTALS
•The low gravity would allow research into substances such as giant protein crystals that would help tackle disease

ATOMIC CLOCK
•The most accurate clock ever made will broadcast the time to help synchronise the world's clocks

CAR THEFT
•Stolen cars fitted with electronic immobilisers could be shut down by a signal from the space station

mistaken, because they *misunderstand* what religion and science are all about.

The purpose of this chapter is *not* to question the importance and value of science. Rather, it seeks to *challenge* the idea that science and technology provide the *only* sure and worthwhile answers to life's great questions. It argues that human beings need *both* religion and science. There is no need to think that one must choose to accept one and reject the other. *Both* have a great deal to offer.

QUESTIONS

1. Explain the origin and meaning of the word *science*.
2. What is *technology*? Give some examples.
3. Why do some people think that science has shown religion to be worthless?

The Roots of the Conflict

Why has the view that science has disproved religion come about? We shall consider two important incidents:

(1) The treatment of Galileo by the Catholic Church.
(2) The controversy over Darwin's discoveries about the origins of life.

Both reveal the tragic results of people *failing to recognise that religion and science have different roles to play* in human life.

THE CONDEMNATION OF GALILEO

Introduction

Galileo Galilei (1564-1642) was an Italian *astronomer*, i.e. a scientist who studied the movement of the planets and the stars so as to build up a more accurate picture of what the universe is like and how it works. Galileo's work has had a profound impact on the way in which human beings view the universe and their place in it, ever since.

Galileo Galilei. ➡

Aristotle

Until the Renaissance, people accepted a model of the universe found in the writings of the ancient Greek thinker Aristotle. This showed the Earth as *stationary* (i.e. standing still) at the centre of the universe, with the Sun and other planets rotating around the Earth.

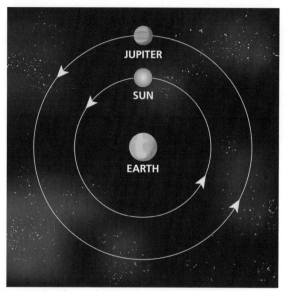

Diagram 1 ➡

Earth as the centre of the universe.

People accepted this model as an explanation of the universe for such a long time for three reasons:

1. They had learned so many important things from the ancient Greeks, especially Aristotle, that they had begun to consider them *infallible* guides, i.e. ones that could never be wrong.
2. The *Bible* spoke of the Sun moving around the Earth. Most people had so much respect for the Bible that they felt it would be wrong to question *any* detail of it.
3. People's everyday experience seemed to confirm the view that the Sun revolved around the Earth. Consider the following story which illustrates this point:

   One bright summer's morning, a famous professor at Cambridge University was out walking with one of his young students. The student remarked that all those people in times past, who believed that the Sun moved around the Earth, were *morons*.

   The professor stopped, looked up at the sun shining in the sky above them, and replied: *Really? And just what do you think it would look like if the Sun did rotate around the Earth, as they believed?*

The point is that it would have looked the *same*. It would *seem* that the Earth stands still while the Sun moves around it. After all, the Sun rises in the east and sets in the west.

Galileo is generally credited with *ending* widespread acceptance of this model which places the Earth at the centre of the universe. However, his work was itself based on the discoveries of two earlier scientists – *Copernicus* and *Kepler*.

QUESTIONS

1. What is an *astronomer*?
2. What did Aristotle teach about the Earth and the Sun?
3. Briefly state three reasons why people accepted Aristotle's explanation for so many centuries?

Copernicus

Nicolaus Copernicus (1473–1543) was the first to challenge the accepted view of the universe. He was a Polish priest who published a book entitled *The Revolution of the Celestial Spheres* in 1543. Through brilliant mathematical reasoning he argued that the Earth and the other planets revolved around the Sun.

Copernicus' theory presents the *Sun* as the centre of the universe, not the Earth.

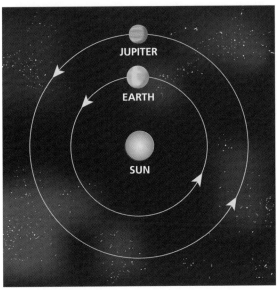

← Diagram 2

Copernicus' theory presents the Sun
as the centre, not the Earth.

Copernicus' book was written in Latin, and it was not widely known or read. Further, he was careful to say that he was just putting forward a *hypothesis*, i.e. a possible explanation. He did *not* say that it was a fact that the Earth revolved around the Sun.

Copernicus did not want to challenge the Catholic Church which, at that time, taught that the Sun revolved around the Earth.

Kepler

One person who did read Copernicus' book was Johann Kepler (1571–1630), a German astronomer. He agreed with Copernicus in all but *one* aspect. He showed that, whereas Copernicus thought that the planets moved around the sun in circular orbits, in fact, the planets moved in *elliptical* orbits.

Kepler's model showed the planets in elliptical orbits around the Sun.

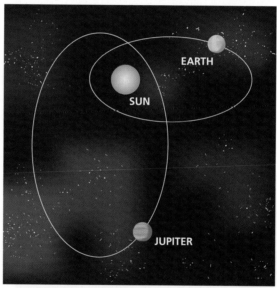

Diagram 3 ➡

Kepler's model showing the planets in
elliptical orbit around the Sun.

Kepler openly challenged the Catholic Church's teaching and he was expelled from his university post as a result.

Galileo

Galileo built on the discoveries of Copernicus and Kepler. While professor of mathematics at the University of Padua in 1609, he heard about an invention by a Dutch scientist, Lippershey. It was called the *telescope* (from the Greek, meaning: *to see far*). Galileo copied it and improved upon it. He used the telescope to make important observations which proved, beyond doubt, that *the Earth orbited the Sun* as Copernicus had said, and *not* the other way round.

Galileo's discovery proved Copernicus was right.

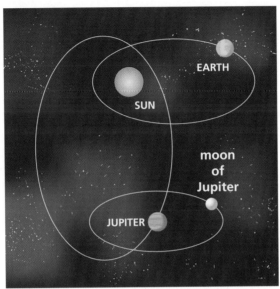

Diagram 4

Galileo's discovery proves Copernicus was right.

Through the telescope Galileo was able to see four objects near to the planet Jupiter. He realised that these objects must be moons of Jupiter because over a few nights he saw that they were orbiting the planet. This proved to him beyond doubt that not everything in the universe was orbiting the Earth and that the old model of the universe was therefore wrong.

Important figures in the **Catholic Church** were, by then, very worried about these new discoveries. The Church had taught for centuries that *the Earth* was the centre of the universe. Now, scientists were publicly revealing that the Church's leaders had been mistaken on this matter. These churchmen feared that people's confidence in them as guides to finding the truth would be badly damaged. They acted out of fear and embarrassment. They made a serious error.

In 1616, the Catholic Church banned the study of Copernicus' writings in its schools and colleges. It ordered Galileo to teach that his discovery was only a possibility and not a proven fact. Reluctantly, Galileo agreed. Later, he decided that he could not go along with this.

In 1633, Galileo was put on trial in Rome by the Church authorities for teaching that the orbit of the Earth around the Sun *was a proven fact*. Under threat of torture he was forced to *recant*, i.e. publicly take back what he had said. Galileo was kept under house arrest for the remaining years of his life.

▲ Galileo before the Inquisition.

This was a sad chapter in the history of the Catholic Church. The Church's leaders were afraid of new ideas and abused their power. They failed to understand that the Church was founded by Jesus to teach *religious truths*. God never gave the Church the authority to teach *scientific* truths.

Although this incident happened centuries ago, and the Catholic Church has belatedly apologised and accepted Galileo's findings, memories of this event live on.

The condemnation of Galileo unfortunately served to *reinforce* the view that religion is opposed to science and that science is the enemy of religion. As we shall see, nothing could be further from the truth.

QUESTIONS

1. What did Copernicus discover?
2. Name the instrument used by Galileo to prove Copernicus' theory.
3. How did the Catholic Church authorities react to the discovery that the Earth orbits the Sun and not the other way round?
4. What did they order Galileo to do in 1616?
   How did he react to this?
5. What happened to Galileo in 1633?
   Why did this happen?
6. Explain this statement:
   Galileo was forced to recant.
7. What has been the impact of this story on the way some people view religion and science?

DARWIN'S DISCOVERIES

Introduction

Until the middle of the nineteenth century, most Christians still obtained *all* their ideas about the creation of the world from reading the *Bible*, particularly *Genesis*, chapters 1 and 2. Most people believed that what the authors of *Genesis* had written was *literally true*, i.e. that the words meant exactly what they said.

They believed that:

- God made the world in *six days*
- God made every plant and creature *separately*
- The first man, *Adam*, had actually been formed by God from the dust of the Earth
- The first woman, *Eve*, had been made from one of Adam's ribs.

Indeed, some people even claimed to know exactly *when* all this happened.

The Creation of Man by Michelangelo.

In 1656, an Irish Protestant archbishop, James Ussher, claimed that he had worked out the exact date on which God had begun creating the universe:

It all began at 9 am, Sunday 23 October, 4004 B.C.

He based this date on information he found in the *Bible*.

Scientists, however, were beginning to tell a very *different* story.

Startling Discoveries

In the early 1800s, geologists who were studying how the earth was formed, began to discover *fossils* (i.e. hardened remains preserved in rock) of creatures long since *extinct* (i.e. that had died out completely).

Scientists began to piece the fossilised bones they found together. In some cases, they reconstructed the skeletons of huge creatures. They called them *dinosaurs* (meaning: *terrible lizards*).

▲
A dinosaur skeleton in the Natural History Museum, London.

These extinct creatures were reckoned to have lived on earth *millions* of years ago.

Archbishop Ussher was obviously mistaken. The Earth was far older than the *Bible* said. This shocked many people. They had thought that the *Bible* could be read literally. Now they were deeply *confused:*

Had the Bible anything worthwhile to say?

Then, a British scientist revealed to the public what he had discovered. What he said completely shattered many people's unquestioning confidence in the *Bible* as a source of information about the creation of the world. Indeed, it caused many people to question if religion itself had anything worthwhile to offer.

WHEN DID IT HAPPEN?

Scientists today claim that:

- The universe was formed about *15,000* million years ago in a gigantic explosion called the *Big Bang*.
- The Earth was formed *4,500* million years ago.
- The first living things appeared on Earth around *3,200* million years ago.
- The first humans appeared about *2* million years ago.

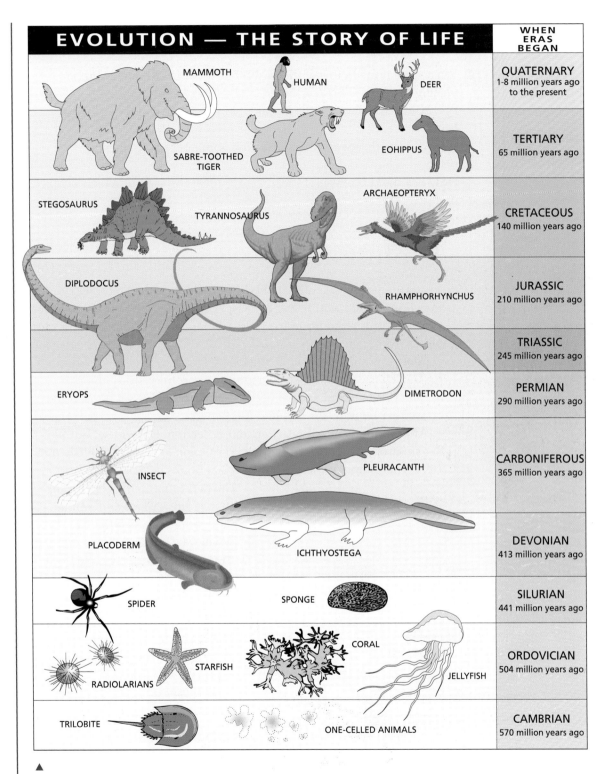

EVOLUTION — THE STORY OF LIFE	WHEN ERAS BEGAN
MAMMOTH, HUMAN, DEER	**QUATERNARY** 1-8 million years ago to the present
SABRE-TOOTHED TIGER, EOHIPPUS	**TERTIARY** 65 million years ago
STEGOSAURUS, TYRANNOSAURUS, ARCHAEOPTERYX	**CRETACEOUS** 140 million years ago
DIPLODOCUS, RHAMPHORHYNCHUS	**JURASSIC** 210 million years ago
	TRIASSIC 245 million years ago
ERYOPS, DIMETRODON	**PERMIAN** 290 million years ago
INSECT, PLEURACANTH	**CARBONIFEROUS** 365 million years ago
PLACODERM, ICHTHYOSTEGA	**DEVONIAN** 413 million years ago
SPIDER, SPONGE	**SILURIAN** 441 million years ago
RADIOLARIANS, STARFISH, CORAL, JELLYFISH	**ORDOVICIAN** 504 million years ago
TRILOBITE, ONE-CELLED ANIMALS	**CAMBRIAN** 570 million years ago

▲

Source: Colin Tudge – *The Day before Yesterday*, Jonathan Cape (1995).

QUESTIONS

1. What does it mean to say that a written account of some event is *literally true?*
2. According to Bishop Ussher's calculations, when did the universe begin?
3. Why did the discovery of *fossils* cause some people to question Bishop Ussher's date for the creation of the world?
4. How did the discovery of these fossils affect the way in which people understood the *Bible?*

▲ Charles Darwin.　▼ *HMS Beagle* at the Galapagos Islands.

Evolution

In 1831, a young scientist named Charles Darwin (1809–1882) joined the crew of the naval research vessel *HMS Beagle*. It set sail on a five-year scientific expedition to study animal and plant life around the world.

When his ship stopped at the Galapagos Islands in the eastern Pacific, Darwin took the opportunity to carefully study the rich variety of plant and animal life he found there. He set himself the task of explaining *how* this had happened.

After many years of research and reflection, Darwin set out his explanation in a book entitled *On The Origin of Species*, published in 1859. This is one of the most influential books ever written.

Darwin came to the conclusion that *all* life – plant and animal – had *evolved* (i.e. gradually developed) over millions of years through a process he called *natural selection*.

By natural selection Darwin meant

a process in which certain plants and animals adapt (i.e. change) to suit their environment (i.e. the world around them).

Those that do *not* adapt are *unable to survive* and so become *extinct*.

For example:
The stages in the **evolution of the giraffe.**

1. Differences exist among the members of any species of animal. Some ancient giraffes just happened to have longer necks than others.
2. By natural selection, the long-necked giraffes survived since they could reach food. The short-necked ones died out.
3. Only those animals with the longest necks survived and produced more long-necked giraffes. This is why we have only long-necked giraffes today.

All of this posed a direct challenge to *creationists*, i.e. those who understood the Bible *literally*.

Until Darwin, people believed that each type of creature (e.g. fish, dog or bird) was created *independently* from all others by a special miracle of God.

Darwin *rejected* this completely. He claimed that all the evidence pointed towards one conclusion:

All animal and plant life gradually evolved from simpler forms. *One species of animal or plant developed from another.*

For example:
- Some fish developed muscular fins and crawled on land.
  These later became *amphibians*.
- Some amphibians became *reptiles*.
- Some reptiles became *mammals*.
- Eventually, through a long process, *human beings* appeared on Earth.

This final point challenged the entire way in which human beings had understood themselves.

▲
Natural selection at work in the evolution of the giraffe.

Darwin claimed that, like other creatures, human beings had gradually developed into their present form over several million years.

QUESTIONS

1. State the title of the book written by Charles Darwin and published in 1859.
2. Fill in the spaces using the words below.
   - evolved   - millions   - natural selection

   Darwin came to the conclusion that *all* life (i.e. plant and animal) had _____ (i.e. gradually developed) over _____ of years through a process of _____ _____.
3. What is meant by *natural selection*?
4. What are *creationists*?
5. Fill in the spaces using the words below.
   - amphibians   - developed   - human beings
   - mammals   - simpler

   Darwin taught that all animal and plant life evolved from _____ forms. One species of animal or plant _____ from another.

   For example:

   Some fish became _____.

   Some _____ became reptiles.

   Some reptiles became _____.

   Eventually, through a long process, _____ _____ appeared on the Earth.

Reaction

In his introduction to *On The Origin of Species*, Charles Darwin wrote:

> I see no good reason why the views given in this book should shock the religious feeling of anyone.

He was being too optimistic.

Darwin caused uproar throughout the western world. People reacted very strongly to what he wrote, or more often, to what they *thought* he wrote.

ON

THE ORIGIN OF SPECIES

BY MEANS OF NATURAL SELECTION,

OR THE

PRESERVATION OF FAVOURED RACES IN THE STRUGGLE FOR LIFE.

By CHARLES DARWIN, M.A.,

FELLOW OF THE ROYAL, GEOLOGICAL, LINNÆAN, ETC., SOCIETIES;
AUTHOR OF 'JOURNAL OF RESEARCHES DURING H. M. S. BEAGLE'S VOYAGE ROUND THE WORLD.'

LONDON:
JOHN MURRAY, ALBEMARLE STREET.
1859.

For example:

■ Darwin suggested that, in some way, humans were related to apes.

Many people *mistakenly* thought that he had said that humans were descended from apes.

Actually, Darwin said that humans and apes were *both descended from a common ancestor* which had died out long ago.

■ Some people pointed out that Darwin *was* denying the *Bible* teaching that human beings had been created *separately* from all other creatures.

They believed that Darwin was implying that there was *nothing special* about human beings.

Darwin *did* deny that humans were set apart from all other creatures. However, he did *not* deny that human beings were special. He sought to explain *how* human beings had developed into such special creatures.

Darwin's ideas, however, challenged the long-accepted way of understanding the *Bible*, and called into question the authority of the Christian religion, which claimed that the *Genesis* account of the creation of human beings should be understood *literally*.

Conflict

Feelings ran very high. At a famous debate in 1860, Darwin's close friend Thomas Huxley defended the theory of evolution from its many critics. Opposing him was a Protestant bishop, Samuel Wilberforce. The bishop spoke at great length, attacking the whole idea of evolution. He ended his speech by asking Huxley *if it was through his grandfather's or his grandmother's side that he claimed to have descended from an ape.*

Many of the scientists present were annoyed and dismayed by Wilberforce's attempt to mock such important scientific work. Unfortunately, Wilberforce did even more harm. He suggested that Christians faced a hard, clear-cut choice:

They must choose to accept *either* Darwin's theory of evolution *or* a literal reading of the creation of the world as found in *Genesis* 1 and 2.

Battle lines were drawn up. Attitudes hardened on both sides of the debate.

Most Christian leaders reacted *very* negatively to this great breakthrough in scientific knowledge. They kept insisting that the *Genesis* account was a factual, scientific account when it was clearly *not*.

Equally, however, *some* scientists used evolution wrongly. They tried to use it to undermine people's confidence in everything that religion, and Christianity in particular, stood for.

▲

Thomas Huxley.

▲

Samuel Wilberforce.

Although Darwin later claimed to have lost faith in God, he was *not* an enemy of religion. He never set out to threaten or undermine religion. Some Christians did realise that Darwin was presenting people with an opportunity to expand their understanding of God's universe. Others, however, preferred to cling to what they already believed and ignored evidence that proved Darwin right.

This controversy over the theory of evolution did much harm. It seemed to confirm the view that religion is anti-science and that science is an enemy of religion.

As we shall see in the next chapter, *nothing could be further from the truth*. There are many scientists today who are practising Christians, or members of other religions. Most Christians today believe that they *can* accept some form of the theory of evolution.

QUESTIONS

1. State whether each of the following statements is *true* or *false*.
   - Darwin said that human beings are descended from apes.
   - Darwin said that humans and apes are both descended from a common ancestor which has long since died out.
   - Darwin implied that there is nothing special about human beings.
   - Darwin did not deny that human beings are special. He sought to explain *how* they had developed into such special creatures.
2. Write a brief account of the debate between Darwin's friend, T H Huxley, and Bishop Samuel Wilberforce.
   Explain why it harmed the relationship between religion and science.
3. Why did the controversy over Darwin's theory of evolution seem to confirm the view that *religion is anti-science* and *that science is the enemy of religion*?

CHAPTER TWENTY-FIVE

RELIGION AND SCIENCE: PARTNERSHIP

Introduction

In the previous chapter we looked at how, since the sixteenth century, religion and science have clashed and how they have tended to go their separate ways. However, it is important to remember that many great scientists were devout Christians.

For example:

- Robert Boyle
- Michael Faraday
- Gregor Mendel
- Louis Pasteur

They did not see the need for any conflict between religion and science. They realised that *each* has something to offer.

Sadly, narrow-mindedness and an unwillingness to listen to the other person has plagued the religion/science debate over the centuries. It has done much harm, confusing and misleading people.

Many people still believe that religion and science should be rivals. In fact, there are very good reasons why religion and science should be *friends*.

▲
Gregor Mendel – his work laid the foundations for the modern science of genetics.

Exploring the Bible

Just consider some of the benefits of scientific discoveries:

- air transport
- antibiotics
- computers
- organ transplants
- space travel
- telephones

With all of this exciting progress, some people wonder if the *Bible* still has anything to offer. In particular, if the creation account in *Genesis* 1 and 2 has anything worthwhile to say to people in our modern, technological society. Do scientists really say all that there is to say?

Christians respond to this in either of *two* ways:

(1) Some believe that the theory of evolution should be *rejected*. They say that the creation account in *Genesis* should be read literally, i.e. word for word. These people are either called *creationists* or *fundamentalists*.

(2) Others see little reason for conflict between the creation story and the theory of evolution. They believe that it is possible to *accept both*. They say this because they understand the Bible in a very different way to creationists.

They do *not* believe that the *Bible* was dictated by God, so they do *not* believe that they have to read it literally. Rather, they understand that the *Bible* is a far more *complex* work than it seems at first glance. It is not one book but a *library* of different books.

Sixteenth-century fresco of God's creation of the animals. ➡

The authors of the *Genesis* creation account were *inspired* by God. The story was *not* dictated to them. It needs to be carefully read to discover the messages contained *within* the story. You will *not* find out what it means by simply reading it word for word.

The authors of Genesis were *not* scientists. It was never intended for people to read this story as a factual scientific account. As a result, people who denounced Darwin *missed the whole point* of *Genesis* 1 and 2.

The authors of *Genesis* were *not* trying to answer the question of *how* the world was made.

This is a question for *science* to answer.

Rather, the authors of *Genesis* wrote their account to help people understand *why* the world was made.

This is a question for *religion* to answer.

QUESTIONS

1. Name three famous scientists who were Christians.
2. What unhelpful attitudes have plagued the religion/science debate?
3. List any three *scientific* discoveries and how they have led to new *technology*.
   Explain the benefits they have brought into people's lives.
4. What do creationists/fundamentalists believe about Darwin's theory of evolution?
5. The Bible is a complex book, containing many different kinds of literature.
   In the box below there are listed the names of different types of writing.

   - Biography   - History   - Law
   - Letter   - Parable   - Poetry
   - Sermon   - Scientific account

   Read the following passages from the *Bible*:

   Deuteronomy 14:3-8

   1 Kings 16:15-16

   Proverbs 12:23

   Matthew 13:31-32

   1 Samuel 3:2-6

   Psalm 23

   Isaiah 11:1-3

   1 Corinthians 1:1-3

   Answer the following questions:
   (a) Beside each passage listed, write down the type of writing it is from those listed.
   (b) Do any of these writings offer a *scientific account* of some event? Why/Why not? Explain your answer.
6. What question does science seek to answer?
7. What question does religion seek to answer?

The Meaning of Genesis

The creation story in *Genesis* chapters 1 and 2 was written by devout Jews who believed that God had created the world. They did not write their account in scientific language because they were *not* scientists. They used *poetic* language. They did this to help people understand important truths about God, human beings and the world. As religious writers, they did *not* want to answer the question *how*. They wanted to answer the question *why*.

As important as it is to know *how* life began, it is even more important to know *why* it began if we are to understand the *meaning and purpose of life*.

The *Genesis* story contains some very important *religious* truths:

1. *God created the world from nothing*.
   This was written to make clear that the *world* had a beginning. Some ancient religions taught that the world had always existed.

   The author's of *Genesis* wanted to show that *time* had a beginning. Some ancient religions taught that time just goes around in an endless, pointless circle. The *Genesis* account makes it clear that time goes *forward* to the completion of God's plan for the world. *Life has a purpose*.

2. *God's world is good*.
   Some ancient religions taught that the world is *evil*. They viewed life on Earth as a kind of prison sentence.

   The authors of *Genesis* believed that since God is *good*, whatever God created is *good*. They presented life on Earth as a *challenge*, not a prison sentence. Life is all about growing closer in friendship with God.

   The story of Adam and Eve disobeying God and eating the fruit when tempted by Satan (read *Genesis* 3:1-24) contains an important message – human beings, *not* God, brought moral evil * into the world. *God can only do good*.

3. *God created human beings*.
   The authors of *Genesis* believed that God is the *Father of the whole human race*. Since all men and women are God's *children*, this means that they *all* belong to the same *family*.

   People should view each other as brothers and sisters in God's family. They should *respect* each other and *care* for each other as God wishes them to do.

4. *God has given human beings a special place in the world*.
   God has given human beings *abilities* that no other creatures on Earth have been given. Human beings can *think* and make *choices*.

   With these abilities come *responsibilities*. People are responsible for their actions. They must *care* for the world God has given them.

The *Genesis* account was written to set down important teachings about God, *why* God made the world and what God expects of human beings.

---

* Moral evil refers to such acts as murder, rape, torture, theft and so on.

Religion and Science in Partnership

Some people still think that science will one day do away with people's need for religion altogether. They are often led to believe this, by the way in which science has proved so successful in improving the quality of people's lives.

Science has discovered so much about the nature of the universe. It has solved many problems in areas such as architecture, medicine, transport and so on. There are, however, limits to what scientists can explain. There is much that cannot be examined under a microscope, calculated by a computer or viewed through a telescope. The scientific way is *not* the only way of understanding something.

▲ The different paths to truth.

Consider *music*. Scientists can tell us that

■ Music is caused when a voice or an instrument gives off certain vibrations (i.e. invisible waves of energy).

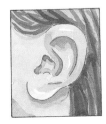

How a person hears a musical sound. ➡

- These vibrations travel through the medium of air.
- They are picked up by a listener's ear. There the vibrations are converted into electrical impulses.
- These electrical impulses travel to the brain and the listener hears a musical sound.

But music is *more* than this physical process. Music also has the power to calm, to console, to disturb, to entertain, or to inspire people.

Consider *human beings*. Many different kinds of scientists can contribute to our understanding of humanity. For example:

1. A *biologist* might say that a human being consists of

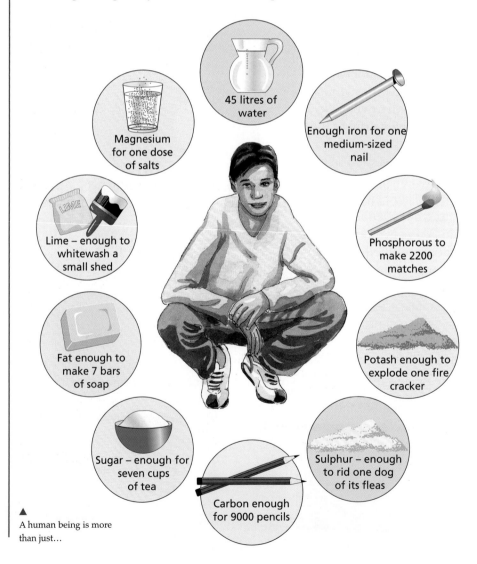

45 litres of water

Enough iron for one medium-sized nail

Magnesium for one dose of salts

Phosphorous to make 2200 matches

Lime – enough to whitewash a small shed

Fat enough to make 7 bars of soap

Potash enough to explode one fire cracker

Sugar – enough for seven cups of tea

Sulphur – enough to rid one dog of its fleas

Carbon enough for 9000 pencils

▲
A human being is more than just…

- FAT enough for seven bars of soap
- LIME enough to whitewash one chicken coop
- PHOSPHORUS enough to tip 2200 matches
- IRON enough for one medium-sized nail
- MAGNESIUM enough for one dose of salts
- POTASH enough to explode one toy rocket
- SUGAR enough for seven cups of tea
- SULPHUR enough to rid one dog of fleas

While this is true, *there is much more than this to be said.*

2. A *psychologist* would say that a human being is a creature with

EMOTIONS	and	IDEAS
i.e. feelings that inspire or disturb.		i.e. thoughts, plans, imaginings and solutions.

This too is true, *but there is more to be said.*

3. A *sociologist* would say that people need other people. Human beings need to live in *communities* and each person plays a particular role in his/her community.

Humans are, by nature, social creatures.

By combining what each of these three scientists has to say, we can build up a more complete picture of what it is to be a human being. But *there is still more to be said.*

4. A *religious thinker* would point out that human beings have very special qualities. They can experience *love* and have an inbuilt desire to *worship* something higher than themselves.

These are *spiritual* matters and they are explored by religion.

We have identified *four* different kinds of knowledge:

■ *Biology*   ■ *Psychology*   ■ *Sociology*   ■ *Religion*

Each says something important about human beings.

Each *adds* something to the sum total of our knowledge about people.

They *complement* each other. Religion and science need each other if the *full* story is to be told. *Together*, they build up a fuller picture of what it means to be a human being.

Religion and science should *not* be in conflict. They are *not* rivals. Rather, they are *partners* in the search for truth. Each answers important questions. But *each answers different kinds of questions*.

Religion and science *need* each other. They *complement* each other.

As the great civil rights leader, Dr Martin Luther King, once said:

Science investigates; religion interprets. Science gives us a knowledge which is power; religion gives us wisdom which is control.

In brief:

■ The theory of evolution explains *how* life began.

■ The Genesis account in the Bible explains *why* life began.

There should be *no conflict:*

Science asks *how* – religion asks *why*.

Each tackles a *different* question. But we need *both* if we are to understand what it means to be a human being.

God, the creator of the universe – Greek icon. ➡

QUESTIONS

1. Science has made astonishing progress. However, some experts in what is called *chaos theory* claim that science will *never* be able to deliver an accurate long-term weather forecast.
   What does this suggest about the nature of science itself?
2. What does it mean to say that religion and science *complement* each other?
3. A new development in science and technology can have a huge impact on the way people live. Consider each of the following key inventions of the last five hundred years:
   - The Printing Press
   - The Steam Engine
   - Electricity
   - The Motor Car
   - The Telephone
   - The Jet Engine
   - Television
   - Atomic Energy.

   Answer the following questions:
   (a) List the *positive* effects of these inventions.
   (b) What were their *negative* effects?

JOURNAL WORK

Read again the statement by Dr Martin Luther King on the relationship between religion and science. *What, do you think, is the point he is making? What important role does he believe religion can play?*